Vickie [signature]

1/19/02

A Conspiracy
Victoria's Secret
of Silence

A Conspiracy
Victoria's Secret —
of Silence

By Vickie Smith Foston

Victoria Lazarian
Heritage Association
P.O. Box 60715 Sacramento, CA 95860

Publisher's Cataloging in Publication
(provided by Quality Books)
Smith Foston, Vickie.

Victoria's secret: a conspiracy of silence / Vickie Smoth Foston.

p.cm.

Includes bibliographical references.
ISBN 0-9709102-0-7

1. Smith, Victoria Lazar. 2. Smith Foston, Vickie. 3. Suicide victims – California – Biography. 4. Armenian Americans – California – Biography. 5. Birthparents – California – Identification. 6. Mother and child – California. 7. Race discrimination – California – History. 8. Armenian massacres, 1915-1923. 9. Armenian massacres survivors – Psycology. 1. Title.

HVC6545.S65 2001   362.28'092
                                      QBC121-106

**Library of Congress Control Number
2001088443**

Printed in the United States of America.

To obtain more copies, please contact:
VLAHARESEARCH@aol.com
Victoria Lazarian Heritage Association
P.O. Box 60715
Sacramento, CA 95860
www.sacramentoarmenians.com

This book is dedicated to
my dad,
my hero.

.

CONTENTS

Forward i

Introduction ii

PART ONE: The Sounds of Silence 1

    These Dreams 3

    Sweet Memories 13

    Map of California 15

    Building a Mystery 29

    Call the Man 41

    Open Arms 57

    Somewhere 65

PART TWO: Only Time 73

    Tears on my Heart 75

    Map of Armenia 89

    Anything Goes 97

    Blue Moon 115

    All By Myself 163

PART THREE: Immortality 165

    Fly 167

    We Belong Together 185

Epilogue 191

Acknowledgements 195

Sources & Selected Bibliography 197

FORWARD

Countless accounts of the human experience from time past to the present are to be found in the world. From all ages and cultures, people have shared their experiences of love, relationships and identity. Vickie Smith Foston presents her personal experience to us a most unique and remarkable way in *Victoria's Secret: A Conspiracy of Silence*. By way of research into her family's past, a past full of dark secrets, she discovered in her personal world new areas of love, relationships, and self-identity which lay hidden for most of her life.

Victoria's Secret: A Conspiracy of Silence also reveals the story of the typical Armenian immigrant. It is a heart-wrenching remembrance of the great tragedy of the Armenian Genocide, which haunts one's memory, an experience the world would happily forget, but something that has affected the fabric of the Armenian soul to such an extent, that our beings, to this day, cannot erase it from memory. Vickie Foston brings the Great Tragedy to our attention in a way unlike any other.

This is also your story and mine, in that we all have the innate desire to discover and relate to our ancestors. Though a most sad circumstance - the mysterious suicide of her grandmother in Fresno - this incident was the catalyst which led Vickie on a quest resulting in great discoveries in her world, which until recently, she did not even know existed.

Very interesting and hard to put down once you begin to read, the universal themes of human experiences touched upon in this book will beg the attention of anyone, Armenian and not.

Fr. Yeghia Hairabedian
St. James Armenian Church of Sacramento

INTRODUCTION

My dad's mother committed suicide when he was a child. Seventeen years later I was born, and for nearly thirty years of my life I secretly questioned the mystery surrounding my grandmother's death. When I decided to take a journey through history, I had no idea that I would discover the life of my grandmother and her family, while stumbling upon and unveiling a secret past.

Within the pages of this book, I have confessed some of my deepest thoughts, my dad has revealed his most grievous childhood memories, and some of my grandmother's most private affairs are on display. Yet, in the end, there are no regrets because what has harvested is the sweetest of fruits; my grandmother's suicide is finally explained, ancient peoples and a forgotten history have been remembered, and after fifty years of uncertainty, loved ones have been reunited.

This is a true story, as authentic as the mind's recollection and as accurate as documented history. However, many of the names have been changed as a matter of precaution, and some scenes were created to reveal reality where specifics were unavailable.

Vickie Smith Foston

There is a certain fascination with delving into one's family history – the uncovering of secrets buried under decades of family stories disguised as truths. It brings out the detective in us; all the more so when your father spends his life in that type of work. But this story reveals more than family secrets. It enlightens us about a culture and people the world knows little of, and it awakens us to the stark reality of some of mankind's most inhumane treatment of their fellow beings. In her attempt to discover the circumstances of her grandmother's life, the author provides us with an intriguing insight into her research, her life, and her roller coaster ride in learning the truth.

Joyce Buckland
Genealogical Research Specialist
Genealogical and Historical Council of Sacramento Valley

This is a journey of discovery, which will carry you through tears and laughter. It will inspire you to discover your own heritage and your family's history…you will see your parents, grandparents, and their parents in new light. You'll want to spend more time learning from them while you realize what is important to pass on to your own children.

Howard Kaloogian
California State Assemblyman,
74thDistrict

In my judgment our people need to tell the world about what happened to our nation that was driven out of its native homeland.

Many scholars have published valuable works about this tragedy from a general point of view. Some individuals have told their own personal stories about that tragic episode in history. But we need ever more of those personal accounts.

You have done just that, and I think that your grandmother's story, which you have recounted, should become part of the ever-growing resource on the Genocide of Armenians.

Arra S. Avakian
Former Professor of Armenian Studies,
California State University, Fresno

Part One—
The Sounds of Silence

These Dreams ...

1

I DON'T REMEMBER BEING TOLD ABOUT MY GRAND-mother's suicide; it's just one of those things it seems I've always known. I do, however, remember the first image I created of her. It was a hot summer afternoon in 1971, and I had just turned four years old. My dad and I had been talking in the front yard for a while, then decided to take a ride on his new motorcycle. We weren't driving for long before I felt the gears of the motorcycle shift down and we were slowing. I glanced around and noticed that we were rolling up to a stop sign. Afraid of falling, I held on tight around my dad's waist. It was then that I began to think of how frightened my grandmother, Victoria, must have been in the last moments of her life, preparing for her fall. I imagined the scene.

I pictured a lady standing near the edge of a building top, late at night in a small desert town. No one else was around, just me standing on the sidewalk below. I watched for a few moments from the base of the building, then decided to get a closer look. I floated off the ground to a height just above where she stood and began to circle around. I noticed that the dress she was wearing, and her black, shoulder-length hair was flowing back from a slight breeze. Occasionally I would zoom in closer, hoping to see some type of emotional expression, but finding none, I drew back to a more comfortable distance. All the while there was complete silence – only the sound of my thoughts.

Becoming more curious about this lady and her intentions, I stopped circling above and stood by her side. First, I looked directly at her face, hoping she would turn and acknowledge my presence. But she never looked my way, continuing instead to stare straight ahead into the distance.

Wondering what it was that captivated her so, I looked out in the same direction and saw the outskirts of this town. To my surprise, though, the darkness had turned to light, and instead of seeing a dry and empty desert, I was standing next to my grandmother overlooking the most beautiful, colorful valley I'd ever seen. Rays of the sun shimmered across the surface of a rolling river that flowed from the range of snow-capped mountains lining this vast plain of lush green grass and array of colorful wild flowers. It was a sight of magnificent splendor. In the midst of the fear and concern that I felt while watching my grandmother, it was a vision that somehow comforted me and resonated a delicate peace and serenity.

As my grandmother and I watched the earth adorning herself, I began to feel a strange sensation beneath my feet. I glanced down to find that I was standing alone, without any shoes, in a mass of rich soil and what I believed was the soul of grass and flowers. I looked up to find that I had joined this landscape. The eternal sky soared above me and the silence of my image was pleasantly interrupted by the angelic notes of birds in flight showering a rain of melody. I could smell the fragrance of the land that surrounded me, each of the flowers in bloom and the scent of pine from the trees. A soothing breeze whispered in my ear as it exhaled over the meadow.

It was a splendid vision that gave me an immense sense of euphoria, and after basking for a moment, I leaned down to pluck a flower from its stem. I had hoped to turn back and offer it to my grandmother so that she might also inhale its breath and revel in the same sweetness of nature as I. But holding this flower in hand, I turned around, and blackness overcame me. The vision ceased and I was suddenly aware that my dad and I had waited out our complete stop and were now accelerating through the intersection.

It was quite unsettling and confusing to think of myself standing next to my grandmother only moments before she chose to take her own life. I felt tranquility in what I hoped she was watching before her death, but I was fearful of her falling from that building top. I was left with questions. Why was my grandmother on the top of this building? Why did she choose to die?

What had just zipped through my mind in only a matter of seconds would leave a lasting impression, with every detail replaying itself like a slow moving picture in my mind. Still, I would ponder in silence for the next twenty-five years.

I REALIZE NOW that at any time while I was growing up I could have asked my dad to tell me about his mother and her suicide, but I didn't. I could never think of an appropriate way to approach the topic. He was just a child when his mother died, and I feared that if I mentioned her it might dredge up painful memories. I would never do anything that I thought might cause my dad pain, he was the light of my life – the purest, most gentle person I had ever known. I think I came out of the womb beaming at him as he radiated back at

These Dreams …

6

me a joy that I continue to see in his eyes today.

So instead of asking, I ignored the curiosity about my grand-mother, even though it became increasingly difficult throughout my childhood. There were constant reminders of her, recurring incidents that I refer to as the 'Vickie Explanations' and the 'Ethnicity Comments'. The 'Vickie Explanations' happened when someone found out my name was Vickie and would occasionally respond with, 'Oh, are you a Victoria?' Usually I just answered with a simple, 'No, just Vickie.' Sometimes though, if I thought it was relevant, I gave the long-winded explanation that, 'I'm not a Victoria, but I was named after my father's mother, Victoria, who everyone called Vickie, so I was given the name Vickie.' Each time I was asked about my name, I thought about my grandmother. The 'Ethnicity Comments' were those made about the so-called 'Southern European' facial features my dad and me are said to have. I learned from my dad that these are characteristics passed on from his mother's French and Italian family, so whenever I was asked 'What are you?' or 'Are you mixed?', my namesake grandmother came to mind again. This mystery woman became the topic of my conversations quite often.

During my teen years I stopped completely suppressing the curiosity about my grandmother and instead began searching for ways to somehow connect or identify with her. When I was required to complete two years of high school foreign language classes, I took French. My rationale? I was of French ancestry (not Spanish, my only other option), and I might as well learn the language. Also, I had been told that my grandmother Victoria's French father was multilingual, so I was secretly hoping I would have some sort of innate ability to pick up the language without putting forth much effort. Unfortunately, no connection was ever really made. I struggled through the French classes, and although I had been complimented on good pronunciation, I wasn't able to grasp or re-

The Sounds of Silence

tain much of the language.

After high school, I tried to connect with my grandmother again. I had become a member of a singing group that later signed a recording contract with Warner Brothers Records. The group consisted of five girls and was ethnically diverse. In the process of developing our group image, we all decided that we would emphasize our individuality by choosing a 'stage name'. Two of the group members kept their own names, and two used nicknames. I decided to keep my first name, but I wanted a last name that would reflect my contribution to the diversity within the group. I chose to use the last name 'Levon', my Grandmother Victoria's maiden name. Unfortunately, by the time the group split up two years later, I had never really experienced any kind of connection to my grandmother, though I always felt it was a nice way of continuing to memorialize her name.

As I grew, so too did my curiosity, well into my late twenties as the 'Vickie Explanations' and the 'Ethnicity Comments' continued. I began to wonder, even more, about the cause of my grandmother's suicide. I was now a parent, and I thought a lot about the relationship I had with my own children and the responsibility I had towards them. There was intense guilt at times just leaving them in childcare for a few hours, and I wondered what could have happened that would make my grandmother choose to leave her child – forever. Why would she choose such a fate?

I also thought a lot about my grandmother having actually existed as a living being. I watched as my own kids grew into miniature variations of myself, reflecting many of my physical attributes, and I would look at my dad and wonder, 'What part of his physical appearance did he get from his mother?' My dad was a very handsome man and in some ways resembled his father, but in many ways did not.

What type of parent had she been? Did she teach my dad to be the wonderful, loving father he was? My dad always made it obvious that he loved my brother, Alan, and me, and we knew that he enjoyed being around us. There were the times when my dad would take us on a two-hour trip to Reno just so that we could have lunch together. He used to let us sneak and play the Keno numbers for him, then split the winnings with us. There was a time when my dad asked me to tag along to keep him company on a 12-hour trip to Salt Lake City, just to pick up a trailer and return the very next day. And there were times when we would just sit on the side of the road at night, directly under the runway of an airport, and watch the planes fly over our heads. Things that seemed so simple, he chose to do with his children. And he trusted us immensely, once giving me a signet ring with his initial engraved on it – a ring his mother used to wear. The ring was the only item he had that once belonged to his mother, and he had given it to me.

My dad was always someone I was comfortable talking to about my problems. Something in his life allowed him the ability to pick me up and give me hope in my darkest time. No matter what the issue, he always remained calm, and it was his perspective on life and on the problems everyone encounters that always made things seem okay. Regardless of what my brother and I did, he never judged our actions, only advised us – and remained supportive of the decisions we made.

I also wondered what type of personality my grandmother had. My dad's demeanor was pleasant, and he was very calm and genuinely nice to everyone. I couldn't help but think that his mother may have been that way too. She had to have been a wonderful woman, because it was obvious she was someone my dad adored, having given me her name. My dad was also a very intelligent man whose interests took him from religion to a degree in criminal justice. I wondered if his mother might have influenced or inspired some of his interests and abilities.

With all of the questions, the growing curiosity, and the image of the building top that I kept secret, I reached a point in my life when I knew I would eventually ask about my grandmother. I was just waiting for the right time.

AN OPPORTUNITY PRESENTED itself in June of 1996, in the form of a college class assignment. I was twenty-nine years old and within a year of completing my Bachelors Degree in Sociology at CSU, Sacramento. I had returned for a summer semester to a junior college, the cheaper route of fulfilling one last General Education requirement, and I enrolled in a speech class.

Having taught childbirth preparation classes for a few years, speaking in front of people was something I had become comfortable with, and I considered myself experienced enough to be able to breeze right through this class. To my surprise, however, once the presentations began, I found myself getting nervous in anticipation of giving a speech. And as I glanced around the room I could tell I was not alone. There were others that looked a lot more uncomfortable than I. Many of the other people in class were recent immigrants, and adding to their limited English speaking insecurities was the anticipation of the delivery of a series of five minute recitals in front of a classroom full of people. Some of the students looked absolutely terrified.

To make the experience somewhat easier, the class was encouraged to relate the speeches to things we were familiar with. I chose topics surrounding pregnancy and childbirth whenever possible or addressed my speeches to people I knew well. However, when the instructions were announced that we were to give a presentation about our family, I was a bit stumped. To get a few ideas, I lowered my arrogant level of confidence and fell on the heels of inexperienced and frightened. I decided to watch my classmates give their speeches first.

Most of the students had interesting things to say about their families and their cultural backgrounds. I remember one young lady in particular who had emigrated from Asia. In her speech she described the barbaric practice of 'feet binding', a historical form of oppression of the women in her country. She showed the class a shoe that her grandmother had worn, and I was shocked at the size – it could have fit a baby's foot. At the time, I was fully aware of the reality of gender inequality throughout the world, and how some countries constrain women more than others, but I had never heard of such a thing – 'feet binding'. I just shook my head in disgust and quietly mouthed a comment or two.

Another young lady talked about her great-grandparent's immigration to the United States. They escaped from their homeland during WWI when the Turkish government attempted an extermination of their entire race of people. The young lady called this event the first genocide of the twentieth century, a tragedy she claimed had been since lost and forgotten within the shadows of the Jewish holocaust. My reaction to this presentation was one of surprise; first, at the barbaric crimes committed by the Turks, and secondly, at my own ignorance regarding this event. I couldn't understand why this alleged genocide was not something I had been taught in any class prior to this.

Other students shared very personal information about their families, and sometimes the audience even cried. I soon realized that each of the speakers was choosing to tap into the other students' emotions. What would I discuss that could emotionally move this group of people? I was married, the mother of three daughters, and I worked at night and went to school during the day. It was hard work but nothing worth reporting. My mom's family (Irish and Cherokee Indian) moved from Little Rock, Arkansas when she was a teenager, to Oroville, a small town 60 miles north of California's capitol city, Sacramento. No real emotional twist to that either. I knew very little about my dad's family – not much of a presentation there. Unless, that is, I wanted to discuss why I knew so little. I could do a story about my grandmother's suicide and how, consequently, my dad lost contact with her family. 'Hmm', I thought, '…it could be like the other speeches, interesting and emotional. And, I could use the speech as an excuse to finally ask the questions I've wanted to ask virtually my entire life.'

Now that I had found a valid basis for inquiring about the past, I had to think about whether or not this was something I was emotionally ready for? Was I really prepared to take the step that I feared for so long might upset my dad? Was I capable of handling the topic without causing him any pain? Was I ready to delve into the past and possibly face an emotional reaction of my own? Yes, I believed I was capable, and ready. I decided to do it.

Sweet Memories ...

2

I HAD TO THINK OF HOW I WOULD APPROACH MY DAD. Call? Write? Or wait until I see him in person? Whichever route I chose I knew I would have to be very sensitive and careful in my questioning. I didn't want to upset him or cause the resurfacing of any memories he might prefer to keep buried. The forty-six years that had passed since his mother's death had not been an easy ride. He grew up in foster homes and saw his dad only on occasion. He graduated from high school and entered the United States Navy. Four years later, he attended Bible College, then completed his schooling at a California State University. He chose a career in law enforcement, working for the Butte County Sheriff's Department in Northern California. My dad met my mom, Ann, in 1965, a single mother with a young son named Alan. They married, and I was born two years later.

But as complete as my dad's life may have seemed, heartbreak

14

caused him to reach a breaking point in 1977, when I was ten years old. He and my mom had been divorced for quite some time, and he and his second wife, Pat, were planning to adopt a young boy who had been severely beaten by his biological parents. Before my dad and Pat could bring him home from the hospital, though, the boy died. My dad's emotional state was suddenly in jeopardy.

I remember my dad calling and telling me that he was going to have to leave. With the stress of all the death he was faced with at work and then in his family, he had been suffering severe anxiety attacks and felt as though he needed to get away for a while. He planned to drive, not knowing to where or for how long, but he assured me he would be back. Prior to this I had no idea that my dad had been going through such a difficult time. We lived an hour away from each other so I didn't get to see him very much. I think now, though, that I may have overheard my mom and her family discussing my dad's condition, because during the same time frame I too had been experiencing anxiety attacks in which I was hyperventilating with periods of unexplained blackouts.

My dad was gone for a few months, traveling across the country and spending some time in Oatman, Arizona, the small mining town in which he was born. When he came back, it was clear to me that he had found his peace. He retired from his job as a murder investigator, and his mind was healthy, his faith revived, and he appeared willing to accept whatever life was to bring him.

Although I believed my dad found some type of acceptance and closure on that journey, I still felt it was necessary to be sensitive when discussing this topic. So, I picked up the phone and, still somewhat reluctant, I called. I explained to my dad that I had been given an assignment in my speech class to talk about my family. I told him about some of the other speeches that had been given, and said, "I really can't think of anything in my life that's comparable, except

for the story of your mother's death. But if I do it I'll need your help."

There was a moment of silence on the phone. Then my dad said, "Yeah, that sounds good."

I thought to myself, 'Okay, that part's over. What do I do next?' Then, as I shuffled through some papers to find anything on which I could write notes, my dad began to tell the story that I had, for many years, longed to hear.

"Well, let's see..." he said, "...Mom grew up in Fresno. Off the top of my head, I think Grandpa Levon, her father, was named Peter. He was from France, and a very intelligent man who could speak and write at least seven languages. I remember him working out of his home as an accountant, and he worked in real estate. Grandma Levon's name was Anna, and she was from Italy. She was such a nice lady. Mom had one brother, Uncle Peter, and five sisters. They were Elizabeth, Angelique, Veronica, Ellen, and Dalia.

"Mom's family never liked my dad. I think at first it was because Dad was Irish and Protestant, and they were French and Italian, and devoutly Catholic. It didn't help that Dad left when I was young, and was gone for the first nine years of my life. Mom couldn't take care of me on her own, so she had to put me in foster care. I was about two years old when I was placed in a home, and I remember sleeping in a crib. My foster parents were named Mary and Al, and they had four teenage children of their own."

Within only a few moments of my dad beginning to tell his story, something from my own childhood suddenly made sense. My dad had talked before about having been placed in foster homes after his mother's death, while his dad worked on mining ships off the coast of Africa. His dad came back to California on occasion, removed him from foster care for a while, and then returned him and left again. I had always presumed it was those few years during his

Sweet Memories ...

18

adolescence that influenced my dad's decision to foster teenage children in our home when I was a little girl. At times, there were four or five living in our home at once, usually the ones that had the most difficulty finding placement. But, now I could see that this was something ingrained in my dad, possibly as early as his infancy.

"Even though I lived in a foster home," my dad said, "I still spent a lot of time with my mom. She worked during the week and spent her weekends with me. She would ride the bus out to pick me up from the foster home, take me overnight, then return me the next day. She took me on picnics and gave me piggyback rides, and we used to go swimming at the local community pool. Before I learned how to swim I would scare mom by jumping into the deep end." He chuckled, "Mom would panic while I just sat at the bottom of the pool waiting for someone to come and get me.

"Mom also used to take me to visit her family. I remember riding the bus to either my grandparents' house, or my Aunt Elizabeth and Aunt Veronica's homes. I grew up playing with quite a few of my cousins."

As my dad talked I took note, and it didn't take long for me to realize that the tablet size sheets of paper I had grabbed wouldn't be enough – information just kept rolling out of him. Even though forty-six years had passed since my dad had lived this experience, or even really talked about it, it seemed as though I had asked him to recall something from yesterday. And, I didn't intend to miss anything, so I made sure I wrote down every word. For me, these stories were filled with new and interesting information. I never knew my grandmother had any siblings, and it was great to hear about the family members that I didn't know I had.

At the same time, however, I was a bit confused about his living situation. I asked my dad, "If your mom was around her relatives, why did you have to live in foster homes?"

He paused for a second, and said, "You know, honey, I've always wondered that, too. I've always wanted to know why they didn't take care of me."

We were both silent for a moment, not knowing where to take the conversation next. I knew that after my grandmother's death my dad had been separated from his mother's family, and that he had to live most of his teen years in foster homes, and now I was learning that a similar pattern occurred even before she died. It was saddening. During that moment of silence my dad must have known I was uncomfortable with what I was being told, because he tried to comfort me. He said, "Honey, kids have a way of adapting."

My dad continued on with his story, drifting around to various time frames. He said, "Mom's favorite song was 'Blue Moon.' We used to go to the movies, and back then the orchestra used to play during intermission. Each time we went to the theatre, Mom would stand up and request the same song." He paused for a moment and said, "I guess it kind of shows where her mind was.

"After Dad had been gone for, oh, about nine years, Mom was preparing to declare him dead. She started dating and seemed happy. In fact, she once took me to her apartment and showed me a picture of a man named Red. She asked me if I thought she should marry him. Then she laughed and said, "...but he turns red whenever he laughs.' It was right after this that Dad surprised us and came back. He told Mom that he'd been traveling around the world during the war, working wherever he could. He also told her that he had sent letters to her parents' house. Mom never got them.

"We started living as a family again and things seemed fine at first. I could tell that Mom was happy. We moved out of Fresno and down to Southern California, to Torrance, and Dad was around all the time. I remember he would sit Mom and me on the beach, go to a nearby airport, rent a plane, and fly aerial acrobatics over our heads. He was a good pilot. But then he started taking off. He was gambling a lot, and there were times when he would be gone for days. Mom used to worry, and she didn't know it, but there were times I saw her crying in her bedroom."

As I listened to my dad talk about the past, I could tell he was puffing on a cigarette. I heard the pause, and then the gasp of air he takes in right before he exhales. During these pauses I wanted to ask questions, but he was on a roll, and I didn't want him to forget anything. So I just sat back and waited, took my notes, and absorbed every detail.

"While we were in Torrance I noticed Mom's behavior change. There was a couple of times that she got mad and became violent. The first time it happened, Dad had to physically restrain her for hours. I had been outside playing and when I walked in the house, Dad was calling from the back room, 'Jackie, come here!'"

I interrupted the story in sudden shock, and laughingly I asked, "They called you Jackie?"

"Yeah…" he chuckled, "…everyone called me Jackie when I was young. But then I got too old for that and preferred they call me Jack."

"That's pretty funny. Sorry Dad, go ahead."

"So, when I walked into the back room, Dad was holding Mom down on the bed. I remember she had this weird look in her eyes, like a glazed-over look, and she was very quiet. It didn't seem like she was the Mom that I knew. Dad told me to get the neighbors, so I did. By the time I returned with the man who lived below us, Mom had calmed down and was crying.

"She seemed fine for a while. Then, when Dad disappeared again for a couple of days, it happened again. One night as Mom was cooking, I stood at the doorway of the kitchen, just doing what kids do, swaying back and forth and singing. The next thing I knew...Bam!...Mom hit me right upside the head with a pan. She beat me all the way down the hallway and into the bedroom. When she realized what she was doing she stopped, then started crying, and hugged me and apologized.

"When we moved to Sacramento, it happened again, but this time Mom was arrested and put in the hospital. I don't remember which facility it was; I just know that we visited her, and it was a long drive, and the hospital sat up on a hill. A couple of weeks later, Dad and I moved back to Southern California. Dad went to work driving a cab, and I was placed in foster care.

"Mom got upset because Dad had moved me to Los Angeles, and somehow she left the hospital. Dad always told me that her family had her released and took her back to Fresno – and that's when she died. All I knew was that Dad came and took me out of school early one day. He drove me to the foster home that I was staying in, and when we were sitting in the driveway, he told me what happened. I was ten years old."

At this point I wasn't exactly sure what to say. There were so many things rushing through my mind all at once. I was over-whelmed with emotional extremes, from the joy and excitement of learning all of this new information to the sadness and anger of some of the circumstances: Grandpa Smitty's abandonment of his family, the foster homes, and the relatives I now had.

I found myself beginning to develop a new, and less favorable image of my grandfather. I was disappointed to hear that the man I called 'Grandpa Smitty' in my childhood had once abandoned my grandmother, leaving her to raise a child on her own. I knew that in my grandpa's younger years he led quite the unconventional, wild lifestyle, with twelve failed marriages under his belt. But I had always assumed it might have been behavior that was only temporary, caused by losing his wife in such a tragic manner, because in his later years, after I was born, he had calmed down.

My Grandpa Smitty, whose only claim to fame was that he shared a birthday with Adolf Hitler, was a very tall and big man, a result, I presumed, of his Celtic heritage. He and his thirteenth wife, Edna, used to travel to the U.S. from their home in New Zealand to visit my parents and my brother and me. I rode on his shoulders when we would go for a walk, and felt like I was the tallest person around. Then, each time he prepared to return to New Zealand, he would give my brother and me some money, exciting us even more. The memories of my Grandpa Smitty were fond ones. So as my dad talked about his childhood, I had to keep in mind that although my grandfather lacked in responsible behavior, he seemed to be a very good husband to Edna, separated only at death, and he was always kind and loving to his grandchildren.

I was also dealing with suddenly being introduced to my grandmother, a lady I had only imagined my entire life as a woman who simply stood on a building top. Now she was so much more. She was a mother to this man that I adored – she was a parent, just like me. She actually had a personality now – and I was beginning to learn that hers was very similar to one I already knew – my dad's. I realized this when he described her by simply stating, "She was a nice lady."

After a moment of my dad obviously thinking of what to talk

about next, and me uncertain of how to respond to what had already been said, my dad broke the awkward silence. "I remember the day she was buried. Dad and I walked into the funeral home and he was holding my hand. I saw some of Mom's sisters standing around the casket. When they saw us they started yelling at Dad and calling him all kinds of names. They blamed him for Mom's death. I can only remember thinking about how disrespectful it was for them to do that to Mom when her brother, Uncle Peter, grabbed me, and I was rushed out to the car. He waited there with me until Dad came out, then Dad and I left. We didn't get to stay for Mom's funeral. A couple of days later, I remember going with Dad to a street corner to meet with Grandpa Levon. He offered Dad money to leave me there with him and to never come back. Dad refused, and we left for Sacramento that same day.

"I didn't go back to Fresno for seventeen years. It was the spring of 1967, Alan was just learning to walk and your mom was pregnant with you. I took some time off from the Sheriff's Department so we could vacation in Mexico before you were born, and on the way down, your mom and I decided to stop in Fresno. It was a convenient stop because we were passing right through it, and I decided it was probably time for my present to meet my past.

"We visited Mom's oldest sister, my Aunt Elizabeth." He said, "She still lived at the same house that I remembered playing at as a child. We talked for a while about Mom's death, reminisced about the times when she was alive and looked at old photos. I found out that Mom's dad, Grandpa Levon, died in 1952 – just two years after Mom's suicide. Then her mother, Grandma Levon, died six months after that. Aunt Dalia, the youngest of Mom's sisters, died that year as well from Hodgkin's disease. Elizabeth and her youngest daughter, my cousin Linda, took us to the cemetery to visit all the gravesites.

Sweet Memories …

"I also found out other disappointing news. Following the deaths of my mom's parents and Aunt Dalia, there was bickering among the surviving siblings over grandma and grandpa's estate. This caused a separation in the family during which his Aunt Angelique disowned much of the family. Aunt Elizabeth referred to it as 'The War of '52', and at the time of my visit in 1967, fifteen years had passed, and things had still not been resolved. More disappointing, though, was that I found out that a portion of the inheritance they were fighting over was supposed to have been given to me. I was thirteen years old at the time, and Elizabeth told me that they had no way of locating me. My aunts and my uncle divided the money between them.

"I went to the County Courthouse before leaving Fresno that day, and found my name among my aunts' and uncle's name on the court documents. The initial 'Petition for Letters of Administration' had my name, Jack Smith, as a grandchild of decedent Anna Levon, and child of Victoria Smith, predeceased child of decedent. It indicated that my aunts and uncle were given the option of setting up a fund for the child of the deceased sister, but by this time, my Aunt Dalia had also passed away and left a six-month old son. The documents didn't state which deceased sister they were referring to, so a fund was not established and my name was deleted from the final documents.

"I remember the assets of the estate were a couple of land parcels, a few outstanding real estate loans, some Pacific, Gas, and Electric stocks, and about $16,000 in the bank. But, it wasn't the amount of money that was upsetting to me, it was the principle of the matter. All those years, I had wondered why Mom's family hadn't taken care of me as a child, and when I came across this, I was pretty disappointed. I left Fresno that day with a very bitter taste in my mouth, but I never said a word to any of them about it. I tucked the paperwork away, took my family to Mexico, and then continued on with my life.

"A few months later, you were born, and your mom and I wrote to Elizabeth and sent pictures. We told her that we named you Vickie, in memory of my mom. Not long after that the letters and the phone calls stopped between us, and I haven't spoken to her since."

It was pretty obvious that the story was coming to an end, as the subject matter slowly faded out. I thanked my dad for all his help and told him I was satisfied with having enough information to make my speech. Before we hung up the phone, though, I confessed to my dad about the lifelong curiosity I had felt about his mother, and that I had always hoped he would someday sit me down and tell me about her. He said, "Well, honey, I did once. When you were about four years old, or so, you were sitting on the fence post in the front yard watching me clean my motorcycle. You asked me if I had a mommy, and I told you that when I was a little boy I had a mommy. I said she liked to draw beautiful pictures of mountains and flowers. When you asked me where she was now, I told you that I didn't have a mommy anymore because she died. You then asked me how, which I wasn't expecting, and not sure of what I should say, I told you the truth. But, you didn't respond, you just asked if I would take you for a ride on my motorcycle. I thought maybe you were too young to understand, so I figured you would ask again when you were ready."

"Did she teach my dad to be the wonderful, loving father he was? My dad always made it obvious that he loved my brother, Alan, and me ..."

Building a
Mystery ...

3

I TOOK THE BASICS OF THIS INFORMATION AND, WITHOUT
fear presented it to my class. That part was finished. But with regard to my own personal quest, it seemed things had only just begun. My curiosity had just been teased, and I was dying to open up
this door to the past, a door it seemed had been sealed shut for
forty-six years. I was eager to know more about my grandmother's
suicide, and the family I never knew existed. What was my
grandmother's family like? Why didn't they take my dad into their
homes instead of him having lived in foster care? Why weren't they
around today?

Now, on one hand, I could understand why my dad hadn't pur-
sued contact with his mother's family over the years, having felt
some type of distance between them. He could never recall a time
when they made attempts to either remain in contact or help him –

Building a Mystery ...

so he decided to just continue on in his life alone. But, on the other hand, I was not so comfortable with the separation. In my mom's family, the one I grew up in and learned from, there was always someone willing to help another in need. And if family members or resources were in short supply, my Aunt Carolyn, a loving lady who called everyone 'Honey' with a southern drawl, somehow always found a way to help. If there were no space, she would make some. If there were no time or money, she would sacrifice her own. Something drastic would have to happen for my family not to support a relative in need or to allow separation from someone nearly orphaned. This idea of a child relative being placed in foster care was a strange concept in my world.

I had so many questions I wanted to ask, but to get more information I would have to look beyond my father's memories. The most logical place to turn was Fresno, to a family my father lost contact with thirty years before. If I could locate any of them, I might be able to find out more about my grandmother, meet my family, and possibly even reunite my father with them.

I asked my dad how he felt about me gathering more information by locating some of the Levon family members. With his obviously mixed feelings about them, I needed his consent before attempting such a move. My dad was very supportive of the idea and gave me as much information as he could as to the possible whereabouts of my grandmother's relatives. I think he was kind of excited himself, and he told me that he would help me with whatever I needed.

The next day I went to the public library and straight to the Fresno City Phone Directory. I didn't know what I would find, with my grandmother having five sisters who probably married out of the Levon name, and only one brother, Peter, to pass it on. But, I opened the book and there it was – my grandmother's maiden name

– Levon – and two first names listed beneath it. Now, the pessimistic me thought that this could only mean that I had two choices to pick from, and the odds could lean towards neither of them being a relative. On the other hand, my optimistic side believed that one or both could be a relative, and it would be my lucky day. I photocopied the page and rushed home.

Immediately, I called the first number listed. When a man answered, I paused for a second (because I hadn't prepared my speech), took a deep breath, and I asked if he was Robert Levon.

He said, "Yes."

I said, "My name is Vickie Smith, I'm calling from Sacramento, and I found your number in the Fresno phone book. I'm trying to locate family members of Peter and Anna Levon."

"My grandfather's name was Peter," he said, "but there's no Anna in my family. And the other number in the phone book is my father's, so it won't help you to call him."

I tried to think of something to ask to keep him from coming to this conclusion so quickly, but I couldn't. Disappointed, I thanked him and hung up.

I sat there for a minute, thinking of what a difficult task it was going to be to start looking up my grandmother's sisters by their married names. Then I thought to myself, 'This guy, Robert Levon, sounded kind of young. If there was a Peter Levon in his family, maybe there was a Anna Levon in his family, too, and he just didn't know it.' I decided to presume ignorance on his part and call the other person anyway.

I dialed the other number, and as it was ringing and I was getting a little anxious, a lady answered. I introduced myself as I had in the call before.

"Yes," she said, "My husband's father's was named Peter, and his grandmother's name was Anna."

Building a Mystery ...

This was it! I just knew it! If Anna was this man's grandmother then his father must have been my grandmother's brother, Peter. 'And I was right...' I thought, '...the first guy didn't know what he was talking about.'

"Hold on for a minute; my husband Albert can tell you more."

Anxiously, I waited. When Albert came to the phone, I said to him, "I'm trying to locate family members of Peter and Anna Levon."

He said, "Peter Levon was my father, and Anna Levon was my grandmother. Who are you?"

"My name is Vickie Smith. I think my grandmother, Victoria Smith, was your father's sister."

He paused for a moment, then said, "My Aunt Vickie died a long time ago."

"Yes, I know..." I said excitedly. "...but she had a ten-year old son when she died, named Jack, and I'm Jack's daughter."

"Vickie didn't have any children." He said assuredly.

"Oh, yes she did." I quickly responded in defense. "They called him Jackie."

Albert paused for a moment. Then he said "Oh yeah, I kind of remember a Jackie."

We talked for a few minutes about the Levon family. My grandmother's father was actually named John, not Peter, as my dad had remembered. Albert's father, my grandmother's brother, was the only one named Peter.

Albert said, "My father died in 1989, but if you want information, four of your grandmother's sisters are still alive. Angelique, Veronica, and Ellen are in their eighties, and the oldest sister, Elizabeth, just turned ninety. Elizabeth could probably tell you more than anyone, she's sharp as a tack." After some reluctance about not asking her approval first, he finally gave me Elizabeth's phone number. I thanked him for all of his help and hung up.

I DIDN'T CALL Elizabeth right away. I thought first about what I would say to her. Then I started getting a little worried – how would she respond to me? After all, nearly thirty years had passed since she was told about my birth. What if she didn't remember the picture that my parents sent to her when I was a baby or that I even existed? All the while, the knots began to tighten in my stomach. Then I figured – I have nothing to lose, and I dialed the number.

After a couple of rings, as I had hoped – and to some degree also feared – a lady answered the phone. Trying to hide the anxiety in my voice, I said, "Hi, can I speak to Elizabeth?"

"This is she."

I took a deep breath and as in the prior phone conversations, I began to explain to her who I was. I told her that I was calling because I was hoping to get some information about my grandmother, Victoria, and I wanted to know if she and the other relatives could help me. But before I could finish my prepared speech Elizabeth interrupted me.

"I could probably tell you when your birthday is." She said, "I still mark it on my calendar."

The knots in my stomach began to loosen and a smile came on my face – that was the icebreaker. Then Elizabeth started talking away. She asked about my family, my dad in particular, and I told her all the basics. She recalled the visit my dad, my mom, and my brother had made to Fresno just before to my birth. She told me that they kept in touch for a while until she received a letter from my mom informing her of my parents' pending divorce. Elizabeth never heard from my parents again.

She then asked about my Grandpa Smitty, but she wasn't as concerned about his well being as she was in his breathing status. She asked in a tone of obvious dislike, "Is he alive?"

When I told Elizabeth that my grandfather had passed away in New Zealand in 1982. She asked, "Did you know him?"

"Yes, I knew him. I also knew his sister Grace, his brother George and George's wife Lillian. As a child I spent some time with them, but they all passed away when I was a teenager."

She said, "Your grandfather was such a stinker. When your grandmother died, he took the money we had pulled together for her burial. Somehow he managed to get it from the people at the mortuary, and they came to us for payment again. We didn't have any money left so I donated my plot. I wasn't there at the time, but I was told that my sisters ran across the grass after him during the funeral." She repeated, "He was a such a stinker.

"But, your grandmother loved him." She said. "We didn't even know they were planning to get married until one day Vickie came over and told us it had already happened. No one in the family was much excited about it, but we still threw her a shower.

"We didn't see Vickie very often after that. She and her husband moved around a lot, and I never knew when she was back in town until I saw her. One time, before Jackie was born, I saw your grandmother walking around downtown Fresno looking for a job. I asked if she had eaten, then gave her ten dollars and told her to get herself some food. Vickie seemed excited to see me and told me that your grandfather, we called him Jack, was upstairs in the hotel. She asked if I wanted to see him. I didn't want to, but I didn't want to hurt her feelings either, so I went. When I walked in I was just disgusted to see that he was still in bed while Vickie was hungry and out looking for a job. I just turned around and left."

Elizabeth talked more about my grandparents' relationship, and the hard time my grandmother had when my grandfather left her alone with a child to raise. She said, "But Vickie also loved her son very much. Little Jackie was her life. She treated him like a king."

The Sounds of Silence

I took this opportunity to ask Elizabeth if she could tell me why my dad had to be placed in foster care as a child instead of with one of their relatives. But, she said, "I don't remember him having to live in foster care. I knew he was in childcare, but that was it."

I was surprised at her response. How could she not remember something that would have been so obvious? Then, before I could say anything else about it, Elizabeth snapped, "Vickie had to work."

Up to this point, I had been quite impressed at how sharp Elizabeth's memory was. She had given me a lot of specific details, so I was somewhat suspicious of her claims at a lack of ability to remember. Eight years of her nephew living in foster care during the week and visiting her home on the weekends, and she couldn't remember? Different scenarios were running through my mind. Could my dad have been wrong? After all, he had been wrong about his grandfather's name being Peter. 'No way.' I thought, 'Something like this can't be mistaken.' Maybe my grandmother hid it from her family? But they all lived in the same small town, how could she? Why would she? Her family knew her husband had abandoned her – that was no secret. She had to work – everyone knew that also. My grandmother's family had to have known.

So I calmly said to Elizabeth, "Well, my dad remembers having lived in a foster home until his dad came back."

Elizabeth paused for a moment and said, "Oh, that's probably just something made up in a child's imagination."

I wanted to question Elizabeth further about it, but she was being very nice to me and helpful with the information she was providing. I didn't want her to think that I didn't believe her, so I left it alone, assuming it was probably something Elizabeth didn't want to have to explain, or maybe she was choosing not to remember that particular aspect of her past.

Instead, I listened as Elizabeth talked more about my grandmother. Most of the information was the same as my dad's. Yet again,
there were some things that were quite different. Elizabeth claimed
that she could not remember some of the different places that my
dad told me his mother had worked. She also told me that her family did not have my grandmother released from the hospital before
her death, but that my grandmother said she had run away, come
back to Fresno, and that's when it happened.

"I remember the day she died." Elizabeth said. "Vickie and your
grandfather were separated, and she was upset that he had taken
Jackie away. Vickie was staying with our parents at the time. She
called my sisters and told them that Jackie was in Los Angeles, and
she was going to hitchhike there to find him.

"Vickie didn't tell our parents she was leaving. Instead she
jumped out of the bedroom window and took off. My sisters called
and told me what was going on, and that they were going to drive
up and down Highway 99 to look for her. I had my daughter Linda
with me that morning, and we had to get some banking done. When
I arrived downtown, I saw a crowd standing around on one of the
streets. I asked what happened, and someone told me that a lady
had just jumped off of the building. When they described her to me,
I knew it was Vickie. I got upset and left. When I got home, my
sisters called to tell me they couldn't find her, but they were going
back out again. I told them not to bother, that Vickie was dead."

Elizabeth talked about how difficult it was to lose her sister so
tragically. "We never even told Mother how Vickie died." She said,
"It was a very painful part of our lives. Our Father's health deterio-
rated quickly after Vickie's death, and he died less than two years
later. Six months after that our Mother died, we believe from a broken heart. Then three months after that, my youngest sister, Dalia,
also died. It was a tough time for all of us."

I expressed my sympathy to Elizabeth about how painful it must have been for them, and told her that I appreciated her help. But deep down, my sympathy lay not as much with them as it did with my dad. To know that his mother died because she was separated from him must have been a horrible thing for a child to have to deal with.

Elizabeth and I talked for a while longer, mostly about her grandchildren, her nieces and nephews, and what they were doing with their lives. I found all of it interesting but wanted to hear more about my grandmother. But, when I changed the subject and inquired about my grandmother's state of mind in the days leading up to her death, the tone of the conversation changed drastically. Elizabeth was suddenly silent, then abruptly said, "My sisters and I don't want anything to do with this."

I paused for a moment and thought, 'You and your sister's don't want anything to do with WHAT?' But before I could respond Elizabeth asked, "Why are you contacting us now if you've had our phone numbers and addresses?"

Feeling as though I was being accused of something, one eyebrow raised and I began to get a little upset. And again, before I could respond, Elizabeth dropped her voice down at least one octave and said, "Anyway, we have enough family."

I thought for a moment that maybe our phone lines had crossed and mixed with someone else's conversation. So I said, "Excuse me?"

In the same deep, potentially intimidating voice Elizabeth continued with, "We have cousins we don't even see."

I might have laughed had anger not already begun to set in. But instead of getting mad, I just took a deep breath, and in one long exhale told her, "Look, I'm not moving in, and I'm not going to crash your family reunions. I just want some information and pictures of my grandmother. I didn't have your phone numbers, your addresses, or even your names until today. Maybe my dad knew your names, but I don't know why he hasn't been in contact with you. It's very likely, though, that it's this attitude you have that's probably the reason."

There was silence on the phone. I thought for sure she was about to tell me off. What would I do then, argue with a ninety-year-old lady? But when Elizabeth did start to talk she was much nicer. I could tell she felt bad about what she'd said. She explained that she was hurt at seeing my dad in 1967 and then losing contact with him. She also told me that Joseph, Jr., the son of her other deceased sister, Dalia, had come back after many years of no contact and tried to get some money that he thought he was entitled to from his grandparents' death. When Joseph, Jr. realized there was no money, he returned to his home in Los Angeles and didn't stay in contact. That really hurt her, too.

It was clear that my grandmother's sisters were afraid I was contacting them because of the money that was left when their parents died. But I didn't say a word. I just let her explain, and then she got very quiet. I could tell she really didn't want to be talking to me anymore. Before the conversation ended though, she asked for my address and told me that she would send some pictures to me soon. "But," she said, "…it might be a week or two because I don't have any wheels. I have to wait for my daughter Linda to come by and take me."

I said, "Okay, and I'll get your return address from the envelope and I'll send you some pictures of my dad, myself, and my family."

"No," she replied, "that's okay."

WHEN I HUNG up with Elizabeth, I sat there for a minute. I think I was in shock. I couldn't believe my great-aunt just told me that she had 'enough family.' Granted, going into this I didn't know what to expect, but hearing something like that definitely never crossed my mind. After the anger subsided, I actually began to laugh about it, then I called my dad. I think he was a little angry at first, and I'm sure he felt the same sense of rejection as I. I also think he felt somewhat responsible for their behavior because he took it upon himself to apologize for the way Elizabeth had acted. I told him that I should have asked if there was a waiting list we could join or a Levon Family lottery system we could enter.

As my dad and I tried to sort things out, we both suspected that Elizabeth's behavior was likely she and her sisters' guilt about taking my dad's money and their fear that the past was coming back to haunt them.

Call the Man ...

4

THE CONVERSATIONS I HAD WITH MY DAD, ALBERT AND Elizabeth replayed in my mind over and over again for the rest of the day. As I prepared dinner for my family, helped my kids with their homework and hung out until they went to bed, my mind was constantly reminded of my grandmother. When things calmed down in my home for the night, I sat back in my recliner. Then, as I had so many times before in my life, I began to think about my grandmother. The image of her on the building top began to play.

It was the same building, the same desert town, the same darkness of night, the same silence. I watched her from the sidewalk below, then curiously rose up to circle her and get a closer look. As her hair and her dress flowed back from a breeze, I zoomed in and found no expression on her face. Then, as I had before, I stood by her side and looked out to see the land of serenity. This was actually a part of the image that I looked forward to; standing with my grand-mother as together we admired the Earth, her waters, and the depths of air. It was amazing to experience such glory in finding myself captured by the soul of wonderful melodies, the boundless reach of the sky, and the delicate scent of floral treasures. I secretly hoped that I could stay there and mix with the elements forever.

Yet, in the peacefulness, I felt there was still a nagging sense of uncertainty. Although I had learned a lot, there was still too much missing, and it bothered me. What I knew was very basic. My grand-mother lived near her family, but when her husband left she had to place her son in foster care. After her husband returned, she began to experience periods of violent behavior so he took her son away. Then one day my grandmother told her sisters that she was going to get her son, but instead she killed herself.

I questioned everything. Even my own suspicions were put under my microscope. I thought at one point that maybe I was ex-pecting too much from everyone. After all, forty-six years had passed, and memories fade. Was I obsessing over this? I laughed at the image of my poor children, watching me and wondering, 'Is she going to start launching into full-scale investigations about who leaves the cap off the toothpaste?' No, I didn't think I was overre-acting. There was something about this story that just didn't sit right. Second-guessing myself was short-lived, and I knew I wasn't going to let this rest until I found out more about my grandmother's life and her death.

Since memories were no longer accessible, documents became my main focus. Maybe I could clear it all up by finding some an-swers in the archives. My next stop was the California State Library. Since the death occurred in downtown Fresno, there was probably a story written in the local newspaper and a copy would be stored on microfilm. First, however, I had to find the exact date of death. No one that I had spoken to could remember it. The most obvious place to turn was the Office of Vital Statistics to order a copy of my grandmother's death certificate. I would have to wait, though, because it would take an average of ten weeks for them to locate it and send it to me.

Once I placed my order and paid my fees, time passed fairly quickly. I became engrossed in the task of purchasing and remodeling my home, and once school started, I became even busier. This, in fact, was the toughest semester to date. I was memorizing statistical formulas, and ironically, an assignment in my Race and Ethnicity class required me to write a paper about my ethnic background. Of course, I chose to write as much about my grandmother's French and Italian ancestry as I knew. Unfortunately, at this point it wasn't much – but as with the speech class I was able to write about what I did know and it made an adequate paper.

Despite all the work, though, I found some comfort in similarities between the requirements in my classes at school and the research I was conducting in my personal life. Applying the sociological perspective, finding the strange within the familiar, to various elements of human behavior seemed to coincide with the mystery I was trying to unravel. I'm not saying that sociologists focus on bizarre acts, but rather that they try not to take things at face value. They abandon the idea that human behavior is something people just chose to do in favor of the notion that instead we are creatures of society.

In my Social Theory class I paid especially close attention to the lecture and in-depth explanation of sociologist Emile Durkheim's theory on suicide. In 1897, he published a book explaining his theory and describing suicide statistics he had analyzed. He stressed that

44

he considered suicide 'the most personal of all acts' but that he was not concerned with the micro, personal or psychological causes, rather with the macro or social forces behind suicide.

Durkheim's study indicated that suicide, although a solitary act, is related to group life. Varying rates are determined by the degree of group solidarity. In a society where suicide is accepted, and in some cases expected under certain conditions, and individuals have *too much* social cohesion, the suicide rate is higher. A Japanese Kamikaze pilot is one example and a Muslim's suicide terrorist act in the name of a Holy War is another. On the other end of the spectrum, in societies where suicide is looked upon negatively, those individuals or groups with *too little* social solidarity also have higher rates of suicide. For example, Durkheim found that European Protestants had higher rates of suicide than Catholics, likely due to what he considered their much more individualized religious ethic. He found higher rates among the unmarried as opposed to the married because they lacked the integrative and positive effects of the group, and the educated were more likely to commit suicide than the uneducated because of the decreased dependence on others and the increased individualism. There were higher rates at times of peace as opposed to war, a time when most people solidify to survive or win the battle, and higher rates of suicide during times of economic depression as opposed to economic prosperity. Also, people in urban areas were less likely to commit suicide then those living in rural areas because people in urban areas tend to have stronger kinship ties. Durkheim concluded that these high-risk groups or people within them have weaker bonds to a core value system, and depending on the importance of various factors, are more likely to deviate from the norm and commit suicide.

But my grandmother didn't seem to be dying for a cause nor was she a member of a society that supported suicide. She also didn't fit any of the groups that were reported to have weaker group solidarity. She was Catholic, married (or when separated living in the same town as her family), relatively uneducated, she lived in the city of Fresno, and in 1950, the year of her death, the U.S. was not at war or suffering economic hardships. Why was grandmother's suicide so different from the norm?

Now that school was adding to the tease of my suspicious nature and detective-driven state of mind, I found time to squeeze in some more of my personal research. I checked through police records, school records, hospital records, birth certificates, death certificates, additional newspaper articles, my grandparents' employment records, social service records, and numerous other records. I also checked with the IRS, Franchise Tax Board, Employment Development Department, the Social Security Office, Bank Records, War Bonds, Securities and Trade Commission, State Board of Controllers Unclaimed Property, and finally, the FBI. I was probably the only person in the Sacramento area who was spending my spare time scanning the government pages of the phone book.

Some of the people I contacted were sympathetic to the purpose behind the research, and I was able to retrieve some of the information over the phone. Those responses were quick – particularly if there was nothing to be found. Most of the information, however, had to be requested in writing, which turned out to be quite time consuming – especially when the issue of confidentiality arose, and I had to send the letters of request for information to my dad first for a signature of the next of kin.

At first, the information that rolled in was limited, and I became frustrated at all the dead ends I was hitting. The Fresno Police Department searched their archives and found some reports from the time of my grandmother's death, but the report that documented my grandmother's death had been destroyed. Hospital records had

Call the Man...

also been destroyed – a standard practice after 25 years. The State of California had no record of my grandparents' marriage, at which my dad laughed and said, "I might have to go back and apologize to all the people who've ever called me a bastard."

Eventually, though, I was able to make some progress. I discovered that my grandmother, upon arrest, had not been placed in a state run mental institution. I knew my grandfather didn't have enough money to place her in a private facility, so it must have been county run – giving me more of a direction in my search. Also, school records were available on microfilm, and I was able to retrieve copies of almost all of my dad's school records prior to his mother's death. On them he was listed as a 'welfare child' (or foster child as we know it today), with his mother's name and employment – as well as the foster parents' name. The information confirmed all of what my dad had remembered, and ironically, the same information Elizabeth claimed she could not recall. Lastly, I found my grandparents' marriage certificate. The ceremony occurred in Las Vegas of all places, three years before my father's birth. Laughing, my dad was relieved.

Also in the Las Vegas and Reno vital statistics records were other marriage certificates with my grandfather's name on them, some of the thirteen that took place during his lifetime. My dad's response to this was simply, "Well, if Dad wanted to get in their knickers, at least he made an honest woman out of them."

ONE AFTERNOON IN early October I picked up the mail as I was coming in the door. As I zipped through the letters, opening the ones that didn't look like junk, I noticed a form with the name 'Victoria Smith' on it. It didn't dawn on me was it was right away, and even though my name isn't Victoria, I thought, 'What is this with my name on it?' I looked across the top and it said 'Certificate

State of California - Health and Welfare Agency

Department of Health Services

CERTIFICATION OF NO RECORD

This is to certify that an examination has been made of the Statewide Index in the Office of State Registrar of Vital Statistics covering the event shown and no reference to this event was found therein.

Name(s)

Lloyd Hartwell Smith

Victoria

Event	Period Searched	
	From:	Through:
Marriage	1934	1943

Ten year search.

OFFICE OF
STATE REGISTRAR

By: ➤ _____
Chief

Date   May 28, 1997

"I might have to go back and apologize to anyone who has ever called me a bastard."

MARRIAGE CERTIFICATES

64849   11541
CERTIFIED
COPY
11-3-49

State of Nevada, County of Clark, ss.

THIS IS TO CERTIFY, That the undersigned ___Ford L. Gilbert___

did, on the __9th__ ___day of = Nov.___ A. D. 19 _36_ join in lawful wedlock

___Lloyd H. Smith___ of ___Fresno___ State of __Calif.__

and__Victoria___ of ___Fresno___ State of __Calif.__

with their mutual consent, in the presence of ___Evelyn Boultbee___ and ___Frances Gilbert___
who were witnesses.

___Evelyn Boultbee___   Rev. Ford L. Gilbert

___Frances K. Gilbert___   Methodist Minister

Witnesses.

Recorded at the request of ___Ford L. Gilbert___   Filed ___Nov 20___ 19 36

David Farnsworth

County Recorder.

wb

"We didn't even know they were planning to get married. One day Vickie came over and told us it had already happened."

Call the Man...

of Death'. At first I was taken back – somewhat confused – this certainly wasn't anything I ever thought I would actually see. Then it hit me; it wasn't mine, it was hers. I dropped my purse, my backpack, and all the other mail and began reading through it.

My grandmother's death certificate was filled with all kinds of information. It listed her social security number, her date of birth, her age, and 'waitress' as her usual occupation. Her parents' names were written as father, John Levon, of France, and mother, Anna, of Italy. The date of death, and the time of death, 9:52am. The burial date was just two days before her thirty-fifth birthday, and my grandmother's stay in Fresno prior to her death was twenty-six days. The informant to the coroner was my grandmother's sister, Angelique.

Finally, at the bottom of the form was a detailed description of the cause of death. My grandmother jumped from a ledge at the top of one building and landed on the roof of an adjacent building ten stories below. The condition of her body was also described. There was massive injury to her skull, her legs, and her internal organs. She died upon impact and after an investigation by the coroner, the death was deemed a suicide.

At first, reading this document scared me a little, becoming more real than ever before. I sat back and thought about how horrible it must have been for those who loved her, especially for my dad. I wondered if he'd ever seen the death certificate, and if he hadn't, what I should and shouldn't tell him. I figured I better find out some more information before I called him – so I was off to do more research.

Twenty minutes later I was in downtown Sacramento at the California State Library, where I found the microfilm of the 1950 Fresno City newspaper, *The Fresno Bee*. I immediately scrolled to the day after the suicide, reading the headings of every story in main the section. I didn't know what to look for – a picture alone, a large article, or a small article – so I looked for anything. But after scanning the entire first section I found nothing. I went over it again, this time backwards – still nothing. I scrolled to the obituaries section – nothing. Considering the death occurred in downtown Fresno, in the morning on a business day, it should have been covered in the following day's newspaper. Then, as I scanned over the front page again I noticed the paper was listed as an 'afternoon edition'. Then I realized that since my grandmother's death occurred in the morning it would have been written and released the same day.

Quickly scanning the microfilm backwards I reached the front page of the previous day. There it was in bold print – **Woman Leaps to Death from Bank Building** – words that immediately baited my breath. Below the headline was a picture, and a story that would forever change the image of my grandmother's death I had carried for twenty-five years.

The picture showed the building from which she leapt with an arrow drawn down the side to show the direction in which she fell, and the text covered much of the right hand column of the paper. The story continued onto the following page with another picture, this marking the building top upon which she landed – and a big black 'X' where her body was discovered. Police investigators stood in the background.

My stomach was tight with knots, and I started feeling sick. But I was still anxious to read the article. The microfilm machine was not very clear and the small print was hardly legible, so I had to calm my nerves for a moment in order to center the story correctly and print it out. Once I did, I sat there in awe with my hand covering my mouth – stepping into the past and basically walking through the last few minutes of my grandmother's life. I read the last words she was reported to have said to anyone, the last thing she did, and

"I want to go clear to the top," the victim told the elevator operator.

Call the Man…

each of the eye witness accounts of her actions. The story was chilling.

My grandmother entered the Security Bank building at 9:30am on a busy Thursday morning. She instructed the elevator operator to take her to the sixth floor, where she got out, returned, and then went back down to the ground floor. My grandmother then told the elevator operator to take her clear to the top. Once there, she went to an employee rest area where she left her coat, climbed out of a window and onto the ledge. She made her way from the West Side of the building to the South Side, where she seated herself and began to pray. Within moments, curious onlookers gathered on the sidewalk below, and people in nearby buildings more than a block away watched as well. But, despite the increasing size of her audience, no one tried to intervene. The newspaper quoted witnesses as having considered contacting the manager of the Security Bank Building, or the police, but after seeing a man in a window beneath my grandmother, they assumed the two of them may have been doing some type of work. Instead, they watched her for fifteen minutes as she prayed, then screamed in horror as she pushed herself off the ledge. Seconds later, my grandmother was dead.

According to the newspaper, the suicide victim, Victoria Smith, had come to Fresno two days before from Los Angeles and was despondent over a custody dispute with her estranged husband, Lloyd Smith, who had their 10 year-old son Jackie in his custody. She was reported to have a court order awarding her custody of their son but for some reason was unable to convince her husband to turn him over to her. She had also been despondent over unsuccessful attempts at gaining employment. As in the death certificate, the informant to the newspaper was my grandmother's sister, Angelique – who arrived at the coroner's office and positively iden-

Call the Man...

tified the body after a description of the suicide victim was broadcast on radio news.

My mind was racing, and I was shocked at what I was reading. And I couldn't believe how detailed this story was. It was far more graphic than newspapers today.

I scanned the microfilm ahead to check the following day's edition for a follow-up story. This time I found it beyond the first few pages and into section B. There was a small story without pictures located right in the middle of a bunch of other stories. The title of the article on the second day was, **'Worry is Blamed for Suicide Leap'**. The article was brief and mentioned much of the same information that was covered in the first story. My grandmother had arrived in Fresno two months before and was despondent over her family troubles. She was upset over her failure to obtain employment while trying to regain custody of her son.

I took my copies and headed for home. All the while I couldn't help but think about what my grandmother's thoughts must have been as she made her way to that building top and onto the ledge. What would drive a person to this point? A story about Jesus came to mind, from the fourth chapter of Matthew, where it states that the Devil took Jesus to the Holy City and had him stand on the highest point of the temple. There he tried to entice Jesus into jumping if he was truly the Son of God, telling him to rely on God's angels to save him. When Jesus refused by telling the Devil that we should not test God, the Devil took him to a very high mountain, showed him the splendor of all the kingdoms of the world, and offered them to Jesus if he would bow down and worship him. Of course, Jesus refused. I thought about the image I had known all my life, and how my grandmother stood atop that building possibly overlooking a land of such beauty, peace, and tranquility – land that radiated the glow of the heavens. I couldn't help but wonder if my grandmother had been shown the beauties of the world and encouraged by the Devil to test her faith as well.

In the car, I re-read the articles as I drove. Then when I got home, I read them again. I sat on the edge of my bed looking at the facts, realizing that an even more disturbing picture was now replacing the image I had created of my grandmother's death when I was young. My mind was still busy with questions.

I called my dad and told him about everything I'd found. I read him the information from the death certificate, and then I read him both newspaper accounts. As I had suspected, much of what I told him he had not been aware of, so he too was slowly becoming informed of the circumstances surrounding his mother's death.

I talked to my dad about some of the things, beyond the obvious, that I found disturbing. First, because my grandmother went up and down on the elevator a few times before going all the way to the top, it seemed as though she may have been contemplating her suicide. What consequences was she weighing between continuing life, and dying? I wondered what it was that enabled death to win the battle.

I also questioned the actions of the witnesses. Why didn't anyone try to stop her? If my grandmother was crying out for help, it sure seemed as though no one was listening. How sad it must have been if she was trying to draw attention to herself in order to get some help and was then totally ignored. I also couldn't help but think that if she were unsure of herself at the time, how different the outcome may have been if someone would have attempted to intervene.

But, if my grandmother really did want to die, why did she choose this method? She had once worked at a drugstore, so she knew she could have overdosed on medication to commit suicide, a much easier route. I don't consider myself a behavior analyst but

I got the impression that whatever drove my grandmother onto that building top that day, she wanted a lot of other people to be aware of it, and she wanted them to know it was worth dying for.

There were many other questions as well. Under what circumstances had my grandmother left the hospital? How much time was spent looking for a job and gaining a court order for custody of her son before becoming despondent? Then, as I read through the documents again, I noticed something. There were inconsistencies in the number of days my grandmother was reported to have been in Fresno prior to her death. Why did one newspaper article state two months, the other two days, and the death certificate twenty-six days when there was only one informant – my grandmother's sister, Angelique? Okay, what was this, a mistake? No, I didn't think so.

I was convinced that something was going on in my grandmother's life when she died, something her sisters knew about and were intentionally hiding. Whether I would find out what that was, I didn't know. But now, more than ever, I was determined to try.

Open Arms ...

5

THE NEXT COUPLE OF MONTHS I CONTINUED ON WITH MY busy schedule between home, work, and school. I spent part of my day educating pregnant teens at a local clinic, while my nights were filled with teaching pregnant women to prepare for a family of their own. In between, I attended school and researched and wrote the miniature thesis required for my Bachelor's Degree. But even though, during this time, I had to set my grandmother's papers aside, suspicion continued to haunt the back of my mind.

In December, I went back to the papers and read through them again, hoping to find some answers or a bit of information I may have overlooked before. The possibility of psychological problems was something I had often considered as a possible cause. But even through the discussion of my grandmother being placed in a mental facility, neither my dad nor Elizabeth, or any documents I came across, gave any indication that she suffered from a psychological disorder. Rather, everything pointed strictly to despair. I wondered why my grandmother chose that particular day to die. Was it symbolic in any way? Or had she spoken to my grandfather, and had he said something that made her lose all hope she had in getting her son back? I just didn't know what happened.

On Christmas Eve morning, I began the preparations for that night's holiday dinner, and when the mail came, I expected only to find last minute Christmas cards from my procrastinating friends and family. What had arrived, though, to my surprise, was a big manila envelope with the name Linda Mason of Bakersfield, California, as the sender. I didn't know anyone by that name, or anyone in Bakersfield for that matter, so I was very curious about what it held.

Inside the envelope were a lot of pictures and a letter. It began with an introduction, 'My name is Linda Mason, and I am your Grandmother Victoria's niece, Elizabeth's youngest daughter.'

I realized right away that this was the five-year old that was downtown with Elizabeth on the morning of my grandmother's suicide, and the other person who was in Elizabeth's home when my dad visited Fresno just prior to my birth.

She wrote, 'My mother told me about your phone call to her, and at first I was concerned. I couldn't understand why you would be contacting my mother. On the other hand, I do understand the desire you have to find out more about your grandmother's death. I too have had many questions about our family's past. In 1979, I attempted a genealogy search, but I wasn't able to find much. I'm sending these pictures from the Levon family album in order to help you to know your family. I'm also enclosing my phone number.

Please call; I would like to tell you more.'

I was anxious to pick up the phone and call Linda, but first I had to look at the pictures. On most I found the names 'Vickie' and 'Vickie and Jackie' written across the bottom and on the back. There were also pictures with names of other family members, some black and white, others taken more recently in color.

Most of the pictures of my grandmother and my dad as a child were snapshots, but the largest picture was a studio portrait of my grandmother. She had perfectly shaped brows, and her lashes donned a small amount of mascara that accentuated her beautiful dark eyes. Her hair was black, and she wore it curly and shoulder-length. She had a rather large, full nose, and her lips were full as well but she lined only a portion of them in an apparent attempt at making them appear thinner.

I looked at each picture with a smile on my face. I analyzed every aspect of this woman I had only imagined for years. I was most excited at seeing her physical resemblance to my dad. The most obvious was the nose, his being an exact replica of hers, and I couldn't help but laugh. And her mouth as well – that was my dad's mouth. The full lips, that exact smile. Then as I held my own pictures next to hers, I realized that it was my mouth too – the same lips, the same smile, and when not smiling, the same occasional biting on the lower lip.

My grandmother was with her sisters in a lot of the pictures, and they seemed like a fairly close-knit family. In some pictures they were near a lake together; other pictures they were in the snow. In some of the recent, color photos of my grandmother's sisters, I noticed that Elizabeth and Ellen had green eyes. This struck a cord with me because my eyes are green, even though both of my parent's eyes are brown. I learned that the green eyes were recessive from the families of both parents, and I knew from where they came on my mom's side, but until this point, I had never known who had them in my dad's family. Looking at the recent pictures of my grandmother's sisters, I was also amazed at how youthful they looked for their age. This also explained my dad's ability to look the same through each decade of his life, even more so, I always claimed, than Dick Clark did.

Too excited to wait any longer, I picked up the phone and called Linda. She was very kind and seemed as anxious to talk to me as I was to her. We described ourselves first, then talked about the Levon family. Linda repeated much of what I had already learned regarding the bickering among my grandmother's siblings over their parents' inheritance. The War of '52 had a terrible impact on the family, as she stated, "It's been unfair for us children because we missed out on really knowing our cousins."

Linda wasn't aware, however, of the situation in which my dad's name had been deleted from the court documents, and seemed somewhat appalled, but not too surprised either. She said, "They're a good family, but a strange bunch at times."

Linda discussed the family's avoidance of certain topics, particularly my grandmother's suicide, and the tearing up of pictures. She told me that she thought it was important for me to question the events of the past, and she hoped that I might be able to get some information that she hadn't. Linda said, "Recently I told my mom that I wished I could remember my Aunt Vickie and my grandparents better. When I got no response from her, I just shrugged my shoulders and said, 'Still, the memories are good ones'.

"At times I fear that so much of your grandmother's life is vague," she said. "...and we might never know the answers. Believe me, I've asked. And in the few times I was able to get my mom to open up, I learned quickly that if I pressed too hard, she would

"Becoming more curious about this lady and her intentions I stopped circling above and stood by her side. I noticed that a dress she was wearing, and her black, shoulder-length hair was flowing back from a slight breeze."

Open Arms...

shut down. I got the same response when I approached other family members, a willingness to discuss certain things but not others. I think that if the Levon family had been a more loving and open family, maybe your grandmother would have felt she could talk with them, and they might have seen the depression and been able to help her.

"The hurt that happened during your grandmother's death and Grandma and Grandpa Levons' deaths will never be forgotten. Personally, I think they have something to hide, and it seems my mom and her sisters have closed the door on it. And I think they'll probably take it to their graves."

I was relieved to know that I wasn't the only one who was suspicious of my grandmother's sisters and the events surrounding my grandmother's death. But at the same time, it was saddening to think that no one had been talking about my grandmother for so many years. In the process of my grandmother's family trying to forget her death and whatever it is was they were hiding from, they forgot my grandmother, too.

Despite her doubts, though, Linda wanted to help with any additional research. We ended our conversation with an agreement; she would work her end and any resources she had, and I would continue to work mine.

LATER THAT AFTERNOON my family arrived for dinner. Excitedly, I showed them all of my grandmother's pictures. I kept laughing and saying, "You have her nose. Look Dad, that's your nose." He agreed and laughed as well. My dad also brought some pictures of his mom, some of which were the same pictures Linda sent. My dad seemed to have a comment for each picture. "That was taken in Elizabeth's front yard. Oh, I was so excited when I got those boots – I didn't want to take them off. I remember when Mom bought those

Open Arms...

for me."

I enjoyed watching my dad reminisce on times he spent with his mother. He seemed happy. Then I looked at my own mom and realized how lucky I was to have her in my life. She offered protection that only a mother can give, and meals that only a mother can prepare. Mothers also, somehow, offer the most comfortable bed in the house, warm and cozy for those fearful nights of storms and bad dreams, or for just simply watching Saturday morning cartoons. And I had my mother, not just as a child, but still as an adult, to turn to when I needed.

My heart broke for my dad. He missed out on such a special relationship and one so pertinent to a person's life. But I was glad to know that the times he did have with his mother, he kept stored in his memory and seemed to be enjoying all over again.

We talked about my grandmother all evening. After dinner, I filled the rest of the family in on the research that had been done and the information that had been found. Since my dad had already heard most of it, he just sat back and listened with a smile on his face. I could tell he was proud of the interest I was showing and the progress I had made. Plus, throughout it all, he too was learning more about both his mother and his father and some of the events that shaped his childhood.

Somewhere ...

6

AFTER THE NEW YEAR ARRIVED, THE MONTHS PASSED quickly. Linda and I talked a few times and reported any progress we made. She had snooped through some of her mom's paperwork and found only an altered affidavit of a birth certificate. Evidently her mother used white out to cover up some of the information, and Linda was unable to scratch it off. I had continued to receive responses to my archive requests, and gathered some new information, but not enough to answer any questions. I felt as though I was coming to a dead end. I had contacted each person I believed could, or would, tell me about my grandmother. I had searched through all the possible records I could find. It seemed I had exhausted all of my resources.

Then I remembered something my father once told me. When I

was about nine years old, and my dad was a successful criminal investigator, I was so proud to tell people that *my* dad could be found on the pages of national crime detective magazines. He was very good, and I was intrigued by his skill. In explaining how he solved some of the more difficult crimes he said, "Sometimes you have to act outside of conventional or methodical means, and it seems it's then that things tend to fall into place."

There was one case in which my dad used this strategy to solve the murder of a young lady whose body was found drowned in a local creek bed. When the police captain had no success in going through the usual investigative methods, my dad was given the assignment, and after viewing the reports, my dad found suspicion in only one person. The murdered lady rented a room in the home of a married couple in which she had her own entrance up a staircase on the outside of the house. My dad suspected the husband was somehow involved in the crime, and with no evidence to prove the man's guilt, my dad sat on the outdoor staircase, at various hours of the day and night, smoking a cigarette. To further distress the man, my dad would occasionally knock on the door and ask if they'd called for the police. Just ten days later, the husband became so nervous that during an argument with his wife he snapped and told her that he would kill her the way he killed the young lady.

To have my dad tell it, though, solving crimes was not a skill he should receive any special recognition for: "You just have to follow what you feel." He would tell me, "If there's a red flag about someone, you have to take a look around at everything, go with the flow, and follow your instincts." In my dad's perspective, this was something everyone had the capability of doing if they would just follow what they feel. And to him it was no big deal, but I'm quite sure the family of this young lady thought otherwise.

There were other difficult published investigations which featured my dad, or gave him honor, one of a merchant marine who had been murdered by some hitchhikers, another that involved a murderer who escaped to Mexico, as well as some investigative work for the Australian Embassy in Yugoslavia. But I wondered, 'Why, if my dad was such a skillful investigator, hadn't he taken a closer look at his own mother's death when there was mystery screaming out of it?' I suspected it was probably something just too close to his heart, and he couldn't bring himself to seek out and face the details, deciding instead to reveal the uncertainty behind the death of others and thereby easing the pain for their surviving loved ones.

So, it was up to me then, someone not so emotionally attached, to see the red flag, to pick apart my grandmother's death, and to raise questions to those who knew the answers. Why didn't anyone in my grandmother's family take care of my dad? What was going on to cause the sudden violent outbursts? Why, one minute, was my grandmother described as a strong independent woman, and the next minute she was jumping off of a building?

I wasn't sure where to turn next, but in June I found the opportunity to follow my dad's advice and work outside of traditional research methods. I noticed a story on the front page of my local newspaper, titled, **"Twins Reunited after Forty Years."** I thought about what a nice reunion it had probably been and how someone involved must have refused to give up on the past despite the number of years gone by. Then I was a little disappointed. Persistence paid off for the twins in the story; why hadn't it paid off for me? I wished I could have reunited my dad with his family. Then an idea came to me, 'Why wait for a reunion to be featured in the newspaper? Think of the number of people it could reach. Why not use it as a tool? If journalists find an interest in stories of lost family members, maybe they would be interested in my grandmother's story. A mother's love for her son, a public suicide, and a granddaughter

Somewhere…

seeking information might catch their attention. And I could use the exposure to reach other people who might have information about my grandmother. Maybe someone who knew her will see the story. Maybe someone who witnessed her death will have some answers for me.'

I discussed this idea with my dad and Linda, and both approved, so I contacted a journalist for the Fresno newspaper and he was interested. It took a couple of weeks for the reporter to interview myself, my dad, and Linda – each excited at the opportunity to share a subjective version of their own experience. There was then a five-month wait, past the events of the summer and Princess Diana's death, for an open spot in the newspaper.

In the meantime, I tried to get on with my life. I began graduate work in the fall, placing an emphasis on suicide for the research of my thesis. And of course, I still had the responsibilities of work, home and family. In fact, this became a difficult time in which my husband and I separated and a divorce was pending. Despite the high degree of anticipation in a feature story of a newspaper, life was quite busy and time actually flew by. Then, I learned of our story's expected date of release only three days before it was to be told to the city of Fresno. Those three simple days seemed to last forever.

On the morning of the print date, I was up and around like other weekday mornings, getting my kids off to school and preparing for my day. This morning, however, my anxiety level was at maximum intensity. I had no idea about how the article would look or exactly what it would say, and because I was living in Sacramento, I wasn't able to get a copy of the paper until someone mailed one to me. So I sat around, anxiously hoping someone would call and tell me about it.

I knew the day would be a long one when ten o'clock in the

morning was my breaking point. I attempted to contact the journalist, but he wasn't in. Linda and her husband, Steve, were both at work, so I couldn't call them. I knew the story was out, and I wanted to scream. Still, I had to wait it out. I managed to keep myself busy for the rest of the day so I wouldn't go crazy. I called a few people to share the good news, ran some errands, and picked my kids up from school.

Later in the afternoon I called Linda, and she had just finished reading the article. She told me that it was extensive and covered most of the front page. There was a fairly large picture of me in the center, with bold print above it, titled, **"Granddaughter Asks Why?"** My grandmother's studio portrait was in the corner, the newspaper article from the day of her death directly below it, and underneath that was the snapshot of my grandmother holding my dad as a child. There was a picture of my dad and me located on the second page with a continuation of text.

Linda told me that she had already received phone calls from her mother and other relatives, each of them upset about the article. She said they blasted me for bringing the story out into the open, with one asking, "What's she trying to prove?"

So, those directly involved weren't pleased, which didn't surprise me, but what could I expect from others? When I came home from school that evening, I found out. Phone calls came rolling in from people whose memories were alive and anxious to revisit the past. Before the night was over, my grandmother's story was becoming complete, and my life, my dad's life, and the memory of Victoria would never be the same.

Everything I had experienced, everything I had learned, and everything I had (and had not) been told up to this point began to make sense. My grandmother's sisters' avoidance of my dad, the foster home situation, and the inconsistencies in stories all had mean-

Somewhere...

ing. Yes, my dad and I were correct in our assumption that my grandmother's sisters were afraid the past was coming back to haunt them, but the inheritance issue played only a small role in the big picture. There was a sudden surfacing of family lies and secrets, and each provoked a recollection of my own past – things as simple and unsuspecting as the 'Vickie Explanations, the 'Ethnicity Comments', the 'Southern European' facial features, and even Emile Durkheim's study on suicide. Most ironic was that the answers to all my questions lead me right back to the speech class from where I started this journey, to one of the presentations given by a fellow classmate.

Throughout my research, I had been disappointed that my grandmother hadn't left a suicide note. But in the end, what I found in this woman whose honor allowed her name to exist beyond her last breath, and whose living acts left me with a lifetime of imagining the landscapes she drew and the death she chose was better than any note. She left a mystery, a silence, a red flag, and a puzzle waiting to be put together. On this day the pieces had been found and fit perfectly. My grandmother's life had such an impact on people that forty-seven years after her death she was alive in them, just waiting to talk to whomever it was that could make their way past the obstacles to hear her. I wish she could have known that it would be me, with the help of my dad and Linda, who would discover that Victoria, without ever writing a word herself, had authored her own story.

Dear Vickie
I was so happy to
see your article in the
Fresno Bee.
please get in touch

Boston.   No

Dear Vickie;
I was reading the
Victoria Smith your grandmother
jump off the Security Bank buildi
remember the name smith, but
jumped from the building and
found out that

Dear Vickie —
I was a good friend
of Vickie's in high
school. just read Saturday
paper. It brought good
memories of our high
school days. I only
went 1 year to Washing
High School

When she leaped
bank building year
I remember her well.
good friend

Fresno, Calif.
in Fosten,   Nov. 3 1997
ad your story in the
e. I wanted to
our grand mother

Dear Vickie
My husbands name is
and if your grandmother

Dear Victoria;
read, with great interest
day's Fresno B

"Maybe someone who knew her will see the story."

Somewhere…

Part Two
Only Time

Tears On My Heart ...

7

FRESNO, CALIFORNIA—MARCH 9, 1950 – 9:05AM.

I've roamed these streets since my childhood. I played softball on this corner, and I walked to school down that street. I know the sights, the sounds, and the smell of every inch. I know that as I walk these two miles into the city the sounds of the cars riding the highway gets louder, and the buildings gradually get bigger. I know the feeling of my feet on the dirt, then the gravel, and finally the pavement.

Each step has at least a mind full of memories, yet still I feel lost. I want to break down and cry but I know most of the people I'm passing, and I don't want them to know that anything is wrong. I'll just continue on at a fast pace, looking straight ahead, and if they think that I'm in a hurry, maybe no one will try to talk to me. On the other hand, if it looks as if I'm too hurried, they might ask where I'm headed, or try to offer me a ride. What would I say? "I'm going to Los Angeles to get my son?" They'll immediately wonder why I'm walking there, where my family is and why they aren't helping me. Then what would I tell them? Nothing, as I've done my entire life…or the truth? Does the truth even matter? Yes, I suppose it does. For some it's important to expose the truth, for others it's important to keep it hidden. Obviously, the truth matters enough to some, in that it is now partially responsible for each step that I take. This, I know, is my truth.

AT THE TURN of the century my parents' left the old country in search of a better life in America. As typical immigrants they struggled to adapt to life in a foreign land, accepting backbreaking, low-paying jobs to support their growing family. As immigrant children, we were forced to work summers to supplement family income. Education and socialization consisted of being torn between the culture of our parents' homeland and the contrasting assimilation into the American lifestyle. But as normal as we may have seemed, insiders knew that my family was far from ordinary. Yes, we struggled with the same problems that other immigrant families faced, but my family seemed determined to complicate the already complex situation. They allowed greed and lies to form the foundation upon which we built our lives, causing battles among the strongest and an emotional tug-of-war on those in between.

I was born in March of 1915, the sixth child in my family. My brother Peter was the oldest, aged 10, and between us were my sisters Elizabeth, Angelique, Veronica, and Ellen. One more child, Dalia, was born three years after I was. Our father, John Levon, was a very religious man with a deep love for Jesus, yet he was emotionally distant from his children and a very strict disciplinarian. He relished control, and in his concern about reputation, appearance, and status, he was willing to walk over anyone to get what he wanted. On the other hand, our mother, Anna, was quite the opposite. She too was a woman with a deep love of Christ, but unlike Father, she lived a life of purity. She was traditional and submissive in her marriage and loving to everyone – particularly her family.

Most of the time, we were a relatively close family. Even when my older siblings married and had families of their own, we spent most weekends together, either at our parents' home or one of my sibling's homes. We enjoyed our time together by cooking; eating, listening to music, and watching the children enjoy the company of their cousins. Even vacationing was usually done together. Problems arose, however, when the contrasting personality characteristics we inherited from our parents were exhibited. The oldest siblings, Peter, Elizabeth, and Angelique relished control like Father, and they too became concerned with appearance, status, and the perception that others had of them. The youngest siblings, myself and Dalia, developed a personality closer to Mother's, having no desire for control or confrontation but at the same time not always willing to submit or behave in the manner in which our siblings expected. The middle children, Veronica and Ellen, tried to stay as neutral as possible, avoiding conflict by conforming to either extreme whenever they felt it was necessary.

When trouble did arise it was quickly resolved, because we all knew our place. This was a family system with a list of rules that began long before my birth. The rules were simply this: Father was the head of the family and was in control of all decisions regarding members of the family. Authority then trickled down through the older children if needed. Family secrets were to be kept just that – with no compromise and no flexibility. We were expected to follow these rules and not upset the balance.

78

MY SISTERS LOVED to tell the story of how our parents met. Father left France, traveled through Europe, learned various languages, and then boarded a ship for the United States. Mother and her family left Italy, boarded the same ship as Father, where they met and fell in love. Once they arrived in New York, Father worked as an interpreter at Ellis Island while Mother and her family made their way west, ending up in Fresno, California. Later, Father came west also, found Mother, and married her.

It was an unusual story of romance for my parents' generation, and I enjoyed watching the melting expression on the faces of those who listened, those who didn't know the story was a lie. My siblings and I knew our parents didn't meet on a boat. They were introduced to each other in Fresno, and their marriage was arranged like most others. We also knew that our father wasn't from France, and Mother wasn't from Italy. Both of our parents were Armenian, born and raised on ancient land, located in what is today known as Eastern Turkey.

This secret was kept hidden for many years, beginning after my parents were married and the first two children, Berge and Berjohi were born. My father decided he wanted to assimilate into the American lifestyle as much as possible and protect his family from the discrimination that Armenians were facing in Fresno. In effect, he changed his children's Armenian first names to biblical, yet the more American-sounding Peter and Elizabeth, his own first name of Hovaness was changed to the American-sounding John, and since Mom's first name was Anait, she was simply called Anna for short. Father then removed the distinguishing Armenian 'ian' from his last name, and Levonian became a French-sounding Levon. The next child born was then given a French-sounding first name of Angelique, and each child's name thereafter stayed more American.

Only Time

"We never even told mother how Vickie died."

Tears On My Heart …

Father was quite happy with the identity change. Mother, on the other hand, was proud of her Armenian heritage and didn't like hiding from it, but there was little she could do. I was a lot like Mother, but most of my siblings joined my father in his comfort with deceit, and as each grew older, a web of lies formed. They began to avoid contact with our Armenian family, explaining to everyone that our ethnicity was French and Italian and that any Armenian relation was due to intermarriage. My siblings became ashamed of their true heritage.

My father never talked much about life in the old country or his family. We knew that he had a brother named Horsut who lived in Fresno when my parents were first married, but no one had seen or heard from him in many years. Father also had a couple of sisters in New York whom he wrote to on occasion, and another in Los Angeles, Aunt Ashig, whom he was closest to. In fact, after Father changed the family name, he moved Mother and the two children to a home on Temple street in Los Angeles where they lived the next ten years with Aunt Ashig, her husband Yervant, and their son Mesrop. Angelique, Veronica, Ellen, and myself were all later born on my parents' bed in that house. In Los Angeles, my father worked as a conductor of a trolley car that ran directly in front of our house. Although I was young when we moved from there, I remember sitting on the front porch, waving at him as he drove past, yelling *'kezi ge sirem hayrig'*, which means 'I love you, Daddy' in Armenian.

Compared to my father, Mother had a relatively large family, though I didn't see them much the first few years of my life. Then, in 1918, when I was three years old and Mother was pregnant with my youngest sister, Dalia, Father decided that after ten years in Los Angeles, he was moving his family back to Fresno. Both of Mother's parents, Grandma Vartanoush and Grandpa Garos lived there, as did Mother's five brothers and sisters and their families. They helped

Tears On My Heart ...

us get things settled when we moved from LA; they helped my parents purchase land near theirs in the Armenian Community, and they assisted with our beginnings in agriculture. I grew to know them well.

MOTHER LOVED TO talk about her family, and I listened, intrigued, for hours on end. Her father, Garos Gianelli, was born and raised in Moush, Armenia to a father who was a Sicilian Army doctor and an Armenian mother. As an adult, he chose a career in Pharmacology, a position of high status in Moush, enabling him to ask and receive the hand in marriage of Vartanoush Mamigonian, the daughter of a very wealthy and prominent Armenian 'Moushitsi' family.

Subsequently they were married and then my mother and most of her siblings were born and raised in Moush. However, when a Turkish rampage swept through the area in the late nineteenth century, killing tens of thousands of Armenians, Grandpa Garos moved his family to the safe arms of America. Mother was twenty-two years old when she arrived in the U.S. in 1901. They followed the westward steps of other Armenian immigrants, across the states to Fresno, California, one of the largest of all Armenian communities in the United States. Mother married my father two years later.

Mother spoke with such sadness when she described how difficult it was for Grandpa Garos and Grandma Vartanoush to adjust to life in America. Grandpa Garos could only speak Italian and Armenian and couldn't practice medicine in the U.S. without fluency in English. Rather than learn it, he worked the grape fields, became depressed, and drank himself out of his sorrows. Grandma Vartanoush didn't speak English either, and she and her husband both relied on their children for support. The year we moved from Los Angeles Grandpa Garos had been diagnosed with tuberculosis

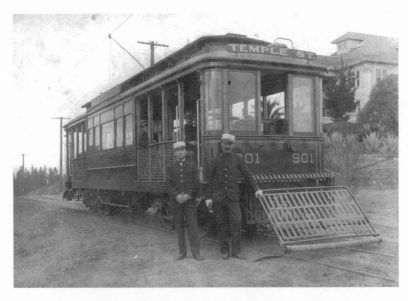

"... arrived in the United States of February A.D. 1900 and my age at the time of said arrival was 24 years."

and placed in a sanitarium in downtown Fresno. Mother's younger brother, Krikor, took care of Grandma Vartanoush – and my father helped the rest of the family care for the property now left unattended. Grandpa Garos died two years later. I was five years old and remember him only faintly.

Mother and her siblings had close ties to one another, but still, some problems arose after Grandpa Garos's death, causing a division between them. Uncle Krikor had taken Grandma Vartanoush to Turkey where she helped him choose an Armenian bride from an orphanage in Istanbul. Before he left Fresno, though, he asked a few of his brothers and my father to care for his blacksmith business. While he was gone my father convinced the others that Krikor had taken Grandma Vartanoush to Turkey so that he could retrieve money from the Mamigonian estate, Grandma Vartanoush's deceased family. Resentment built toward Uncle Krikor while he was gone and little care was taken of his blacksmith shop. When he, his new bride, and Grandma Vartanoush returned from Turkey, he found that his business had failed, and all of his supplies were gone. Uncle Krikor denied that he and Grandma Vartanoush received any money while in Turkey, but few believed him. Uncle Krikor also confronted Father about missing equipment and items from the blacksmith shop. Father told Uncle Krikor that he sold the items in order to be compensated for the inconvenience of tending to an unprofitable business. Disgusted, Uncle Krikor moved his new wife and Grandma Vartanoush to San Francisco. Minimal contact was kept with them.

MOTHER HAD SUCH pride in her heritage. She loved to sit in her rocking chair on the front porch and tell stories of her homeland. She talked about the three thousand years that Armenians occupied and cherished the most beautiful of lands – with snow-capped

Tears On My Heart ...

mountains, the scent of pine, the massive river valleys, and a medley of colorful flowers. It was these images at such a young age that sparked my interest in art, and a desire to draw landscapes in charcoal and mountainous valley paintings. I drew pictures of what I dreamt of visiting, Armenia, smelling the forest and the flowers Mother described, hearing the sounds of the rushing rivers she adored, standing in a field of flowers as a breeze whispered in my ear.

She also spoke with pride of the adversities the Armenians faced and obstacles overcome throughout their history. She told me that Noah's Ark alighted on Mt. Ararat, and when his family descended from the mountain and scattered throughout the world, some remained at the base of the mountain. That group of people later mixed with migrants from Asia, Aryans from the Northeast, and Greeks from Thrace in the West. This combination became what we know of today as the Armenian people. Mt. Ararat, she said, continues to be the most treasured of mountains for the Armenians, and today still holds the remains of the Ark—remains that Mother says God has forbidden anyone from reaching and removing.

Mother told me that there had been periods of massive Armenian kingdoms that spread throughout the land between the Black, the Caspian, and the Mediterranean Seas. Because of this, however, and the ideal location of Armenian land in the center of the trade route between Europe and Asia, Armenians were also constantly invaded, and at times they lost power or land to their intruders. The most significant of troubles for Armenians as Mother described, was not due to their land, though, and began in 301 AD. Armenian King, Tiridates III, who practiced paganism, had fallen in love with a Christian girl. When she refused the offer to be his queen, he had her killed. King Tiridates then went insane; a result, it was believed, of the crime he had committed. Gregory, a man the king had imprisoned in a dungeon eleven years prior because of his devout faith in Christianity, was brought by his follows to heal the king. When King Tiridates saw Gregory, he was shocked that Gregory was still alive. The King considered Gregory's survival in the dungeon a miracle and the King's sanity was regained; he embraced Christianity, and then adopted it as his state's national religion. Armenia became the first Christian nation in the world, followed by the Romans eleven years later. Armenia also became the minority among predominantly non-Christian neighboring countries, and began suffering constant persecution.

Mother told a story of her mother's ancestors, the Mamigonian family, and their famous battle in 451 AD. A Persian ruler, Yazdegerd, had tried to force the Armenians to give up their Christian beliefs and accept Zoroasterism, and his troops invaded the land. But Armenian men, women, and children refused to abandon their religion. Although outnumbered, they fought the Persians. It was a battle led first by General Vardan Mamigonian until he was killed, then by his nephew, Vahaan Mamigonian, who led the people in war until the Persians retreated thirty-three years later. Armenians were able to keep their Christian faith, and Vahaan Mamigonian, with his family's winter home in Moush, ruled as Prince of Armenia until his death – leaving the 'Moushitsi Mamigonian' family with great wealth for the next 1500 years, the family into which Grandmother Vartanoush was born.

Despite the Armenian's success against the Persians, religious persecution continued. The most destructive events occurred during the eleventh century when barbaric Muslim Seljuk Turks began filtering into Asia Minor. Armenian land was slowly overrun, and by the sixteenth century, the Muslim Ottoman Turks finally conquered all Armenian territory. Any Christians on the land, mostly Greeks and Armenians, were forced into a life as second class citizens.

There they lived for hundreds of years as loyal millet in the Muslim ruled Ottoman Empire. But despite their submission and loyalty to the Turks, persecution against Christians worsened, and for the Armenians, this often came in the form of massacre. From 1894-1896, the Turks killed thousands of Armenians in and around the city of Moush. It was this fear of continued barbarism that led Grandpa Garos to move his family to the United States.

Mother told me that even after she moved and things calmed some, brutality toward Armenians in the Ottoman Empire continued. Muslims had long despised Christians, and the Armenian Christians in particular because of their number: over two million people. Fourteen years after Mother's family moved to America, during WWI, the Turks had hoped to join Germany and Iraq in building a Baghdad to Berlin railway. But there was a problem; it would have to run through the densely populated Armenian land. Also during the war the Turks, allies with Germany, feared the Christian Armenians might conspire with enemy Christian nations, particularly the Russians. So, in 1915, the year of my birth, the Turkish government began what they called the 'Final Solution' to the question of the Armenians. We now refer to it as the Armenian Genocide.

In February, when the Turks believed the world was preoccupied with the WWI, they claimed 'jihad' or holy war against the Christians in the Ottoman Empire. They forced the Greeks into the Mediterranean Sea to sink or swim to awaiting vessels, while forcing others back to Greece by land and killing the rest. The Turks then began a systematic destruction of the entire Armenian race. In March, the month that I was born, *The New York Times* began running stories of the atrocities committed against helpless Armenians. But despite the sympathy expressed, the world did little to help

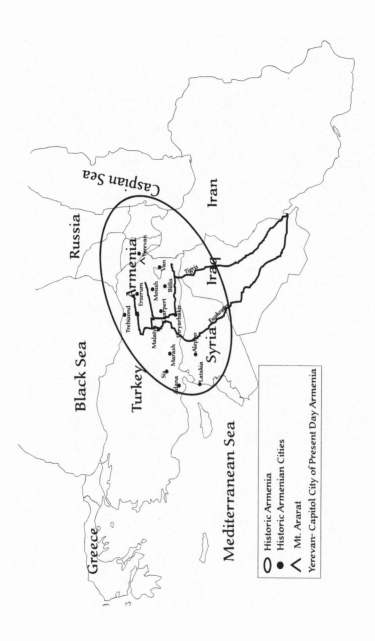

Historic Armenia
Historic Armenian Cities
Mt. Ararat
Yerevan- Capitol City of Present Day Armenia

and less than a year later 1.5 million Armenians had been shot, drowned, burned, raped, stabbed, or marched through the desert to their death. The rest escaped into exile through neighboring countries. Grandma Vartanoush's Mamigonian family, their wealth and their legacy, was gone, as were the souls of three-fourths of the Armenian population, destroyed at the hands of the Turks.

MANY SURVIVORS OF the Genocide worked their way toward the United States, and since Fresno was one of the few cities in America that already had a fairly large Armenian community, many came here. My youngest years are imprinted with images of destroyed families virtually crawling into our community. Widows were caring for each other and for orphans, and orphans were caring for siblings and friends. It broke my heart to watch these families in such despair, but worse yet were the stories brought with them.

When I was eight years old, I listened as some of my cousins and a group of other local kids gathered in a nearby field, telling stories about the Genocide. They started with the village massacres and one of our neighbors, Mrs. Kabajian. "She was forced..." one boy said, "...from her home during a midnight raid on her village. She watched as the Turkish soldiers, or gendarmes as they and the Turkish police were called, led Armenian men away from town. Those men were never seen again. Anyone remaining in the village, mostly women, children, and the elderly, were forced with their belongings onto a mule driven cart, or made to walk out of the village with whatever they could carry, into the snow-packed mountains. Women and girls were also raped and the village was torn apart. Mrs. Kabajian watched as her sister, Dirouhi, was thrown into a burning church, then with her body afire, ran out of the flames screaming for help. She was shot in the head."

The boy told that as the Turks lined Armenians up in the streets, they began to confiscate their belongings, keeping money and food.

"Mrs. Kabajian saw an old man resist the gendarmes aggression, so they beat him. And when they noticed a tattoo of a cross on the old man's wrist, they cut off his arm."

I had learned from my mother's stories that this tattoo was a tradition among Armenians, who have at least once in their lifetime made a pilgrimage to Jerusalem, so I knew what this meant. As the faces of some of the other children looked on curiously, I leaned over to one of my friends and whispered, "Jerusalem Pilgrimage," receiving a nod of her head in confirmation.

"The Turks left that old man lying in the snow to die." The boy continued, "They set the entire village on fire and escorted the caravan into the mountains."

Mrs. Kabajian was a widow, for all she knew, who hadn't seen her husband since the Turks took him from her village in Erzerum that day. In Fresno, she lived a very quiet life, singing melancholy songs to herself and rarely speaking a word to anyone. From that day forth, each time I saw Mrs. Kabajian, my heart wept for her.

Another boy in the group talked about the children of the genocide. "Young girls who didn't escape and weren't raped or killed by Turks and Kurds were taken as slaves into harems or married off to Turkish men – forced to convert from Christianity to Islam and deny their heritage. Young boys were taken and raised by Turks, forced to serve in the Turkish military and claim Turk ancestry. But quite often the children were simply killed, tossed into pits and covered by rocks, forced into caves and suffocated, or intentionally drowned. There were some incidents in the Black Sea off the coast of Trebizond. Armenian children were loaded onto boats wearing nothing but t-shirts, set out to sea, and in view of their mothers watching helplessly from the shoreline, the boats were capsized. Thousands of terrified children clutched onto one another as they drowned in swarms. For the young who tried to swim back to shore or mothers who tried to save their children, there was a gendarme waiting in a nearby boat to end their struggle for life with a bullet."

Being a child myself at the time, and unable to swim, I remember being terribly frightened by these accounts. I feared for many years afterwards that the Turks might invade the U.S., find me, and force my fate in the same mode of slaughter.

The last story I remember being told that day concerned a schoolmate of my older sisters', a girl named Araxi, and how she had been forced from her home in Bitlis.

"The deportation, as the Turks called it, consisted of Armenians walking in caravans through the desert..." one girl said, "...led by Turkish police and soldiers, and even the Kurds, into Aleppo, Syria. Many of those who didn't starve to death or die of thirst along the way were killed while marching. Only the strong and lucky survived.

"Araxi's mother had been killed, and she herself survived by dressing as a young boy escorting younger siblings along the path. But Araxi witnessed many horrors that continued to haunt her still. She watched as an Armenian priest that walked with them, blessing the dead and dying bodies they passed, was knocked down and held to the ground by the gendarmes. Then, as he screamed in pain, horseshoes were nailed to the bottom of his feet. The gendarmes lifted the priest to a stand and at gunpoint ordered him to dance. When the priest struggled to his feet and attempted to move his legs, the soldiers laughed. When he collapsed, they shot him."

"As Araxi continued walking, she watched in horror as her best friend, Haygouhi, was attacked. Haygouhi was a beautiful ten-year old Armenian girl with magnificent green eyes. The gendarmes found her attractive. They often harassed and teased her by stroking her face and hair. Frightened, Haygouhi tried to avoid them by simply marching on. Having witnessed the rape and murder of other young girls and women, Haygouhi was aware of what possibly awaited her, and sure enough her fate was sealed. After two weeks of marching through the wretched heat with the terrorizing and tormenting Turkish soldiers, Haygouhi was snatched from the deportation line, shoved to the ground, and in front of those marching past, a gendarme raped and beat her. Araxi, still dressed as a boy, could do nothing but look straight ahead and try to avoid watching or hearing her friend's pleas for help. A sympathetic, old Turkish lady who heard Haygouhi's cries ran from a nearby field screaming and hit the soldier. She too was beaten. The gendarme then stood up and spat upon Haygouhi, as she lay balled in shame with her face in the dirt. Araxi never saw her friend again and believes Haygouhi probably chose to lie there and die."

This story was particularly disturbing to me because my sisters Elizabeth and Ellen were both green-eyed Armenian girls. It was a rare trait to carry, for most Armenians had dark features, but in my family Elizabeth and Ellen were the bearers of these unique characteristics. I also couldn't help but think that Haygouhi was the same age as my sister Ellen, and it sickened me to think of her ever having to endure such a dreadful ordeal.

"As Araxi marched on," the girl told, "she saw men approaching on horseback. Stories had been told about men being released from prison by the Turkish government, armed, and sent to kill the Armenians that walked through the lands. Araxi became frightened, and when the others noticed these men approaching, panic erupted. Those strong enough to run scattered in all directions. Many of the mothers dashed toward the river and tossed their children in, having them drown as opposed to face a brutal death at the hands of these men. Some of these women were then cut down for their defiance. One lady didn't run at all; she simply walked on with her child wrapped onto her back. This lady was unaware that one of the barbarians on horseback had passed behind and cut off her child's head. When she discovered it a short time later, she screamed in horror, running in circles, and dropping to her knees, praying to God. The gendarmes then killed the grieving mother.

"Those who survived the organized attacks, the starvation, the heat, and the rape and murder were marched on and eventually placed into cattle cars. They were transported to the next deportation site where they were paraded further, eventually reaching refugee camps in Aleppo, Syria, disease ridden but safe in the auspices of the American Red Cross."

I was lost in the stories as if they were my own. I'm sure this group of family and friends had no idea of the impact these images would have on my life. They angered me enough to want to preserve my heritage, if for no other reason than simply to prove our resilience to the Turks. But in my situation it wasn't as simple as that, so although I was restricted from becoming actively involved in Armenian related activities, I learned to jostle the limits within my family without crossing over the line.

To add insult to the 'Genocide Armenian's' injury, once they arrived in Fresno they had to endure further hardships. They joined the already established Armenian immigrants in facing discrimination, as natives teased us for our olive colored skin, called us low class Jews or damn Turks, and at school referred to us as 'you foreign children.' The 'Genocide Armenians' joined us in feeling the pressures of assimilation, where we were encouraged to change our habits, our foods, our culture, and our names. And still, despite any attempts at change, we were forced to live in the stench of sewage, forbidden by a covenant in real estate deeds to purchase land in any other city sector. But, I was proud to see the 'Genocide Arme-

nians' respond as our families had, by putting forth their efforts in
overcoming their past by using their education, along with backbreaking grunt work to slowly rebuild their lives.

By the end of WWI, Ancient Armenia and its' people were basically ruined. The few who managed to survive in Turkey did so
under harsh conditions, while others faced adversities in their
adopted lands. The Allies victory in the war allotted Armenians a
small area of their ancient homeland to call their own, with the un-
fortunate site of Mt. Ararat sitting on the opposite side of the Armenian boarder, in Turkey. But, the United State refused to accept the
mandate for the Middle East during post-war negotiations, and
Armenia had no one to help them establish a self-sufficient country.
So instead of prospering, within two years the Armenian State was
faced with invasion of the Turks on their Western border, with no
ability to resist, and an offer by the USSR to become a fellow Republic. The Armenian government was forced into accepting the lesser
of the two evils, and the Russians invaded.

The Genocide and fear of Russian influence diluting the Armenian culture sparked a renewal of pride in Armenians around the
world. It clearly happened in my mother's family. In 1925, when I
was ten years old, I accompanied Mother to her sister's house almost everyday for months, where she and my aunts made a picture
out of beads. When it was complete the picture showed a lady sitting in ruins, and the land around the lady was labeled as ancient
Armenian cities. This picture was called 'Mother Armenia', and at
the bottom it was written, 'Always love your Motherland'. It won
first place in the Fresno County fair that year, and later given as a
gift to Grandma Vartanoush. She died in 1926, and we have been
told that Uncle Krikor has this picture hanging in his home today.

Anything Goes ...

8

THROUGHOUT MOST OF MY EARLY CHILDHOOD I WAS COM-
fortably embraced in the arms of my Armenian mother. She cooked
mostly Armenian food and spoke the Armenian language (broken
English only when necessary). My siblings and I spoke only Armenian until we entered the American school system. But difficulty
came in explaining to my siblings why, as I was growing older, I
wasn't avoiding my heritage as they were. It frightened them to
think that their claims to French and Italian ancestry might be ex-
posed as a lie by my contact with Armenians. My sisters had joined
the Anglo locals with the general consensus, disgusted with Armenian culture and lifestyle. My siblings lived a ritzy air, believing
they were somehow superior to the Armenians. Each dreamed of
marrying an *odar* (non-Armenian), not just for love, but one who
would rescue them from the ghetto. Each of their wishes eventually
came true.

There were times when my sisters tried to convince me that my
life held more prospects if I didn't associate with Armenians, and

when that didn't change my behavior, they tried to bully me. They held me down once and cut my hair, hair they said had a texture and a style that was too similar to the Armenians – saying it was for my own good. My sisters then told me that if my relationships with Armenians were to continue, they might be forced to avoid me the way they avoided our other Armenian relatives. Each then turned the blame on Mother for my continued interest in the Armenians, telling her that she could no longer speak Armenian when they or their guests were around. Angelique said, "Mother, if you're not going to speak English, then don't speak at all."

And so Mother didn't. She became very quiet when people were around. I know it broke her heart to see her children so ashamed of their heritage, but she never said a word to them about it. She loved her children despite their shortcomings. For me, it was terribly disappointing to see my siblings act in such a way, but I felt they were entitled to their own lifestyle and should live however they chose without coercion from anyone. At the same time, I also thought they should show Mother and me the same respect. In the end, it was never given, but I loved and respected family and the times we shared together. I didn't want to jeopardize that, so, like Mother, I didn't say anything to them either.

IN 1936, I was twenty-one years old. Most of my siblings were married, Peter to a Portuguese lady, and Elizabeth, Angelique, and Veronica to *odars*. Ellen, Dalia, and I dated some but hadn't found suitable partners. I really enjoyed playing practical jokes on my nieces and nephews, and I hoped to have a family of my own some day. I certainly felt the pressures from my family, and society in general, to find a husband, become a good wife, and raise a family. But the '30's were the Depression Era, and although food prices dropped some, there weren't a lot of men, Armenian or *odar*, seek-

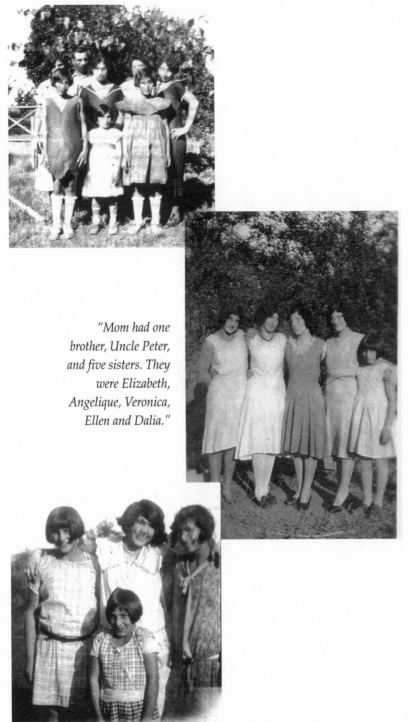

"Mom had one brother, Uncle Peter, and five sisters. They were Elizabeth, Angelique, Veronica, Ellen and Dalia."

Anything Goes ...

"Our gang having a snow party."

"She was a nice lady. "

Anything Goes …

ing brides or families they couldn't afford to feed. Instead, I drew my charcoal landscapes and painted the lush valleys of Armenia described to me by my mother while completing Beautician College with my sisters Veronica and Ellen.

My sisters and I were now all adults, but still we spent a lot of time together at Elizabeth's house. We used to hang out on the front porch watching the children play with their cousins, then listened to the Big Show over the radio at night. With a thirteen-year gap between the oldest and youngest of us sisters, one of the favorite things to do was compare the hottest entertainers from each generation. Elizabeth, Angelique, and Veronica loved the 1920's, the silent movies and Charlie Chaplin, Burns and Allen in vaudeville, Rudolph Valentino, Greta Garbo, and Douglas Fairbanks. Ellen, Dalia and I adored the 1930's love stories and musicals: Clark Gable, James Cagney, Fred Astaire, Ginger Rogers, and that cute little Shirley Temple. I think we had all become romantics at heart, only stimulated by different eras. Listening to the phonograph, we used to dance the Charleston, the jitterbug, and the conga, sing the blues, and dress up and character play. It was a nice release for us, having grown up in a conservative environment, sheltered from many worldly activities.

Our parents' home was strictly Christian. My father and mother were married in the Holy Trinity Armenian Apostolic Church in downtown Fresno. They attended church there until father changed the Armenian last name and decided to limit his ties to Armenians. Mother told me that she and father attempted to attend a couple of non-Armenian, orthodox churches, but members of the congregation who knew they were Armenian made it clear that my family was not wanted there. At the time Armenians were being turned away, forced to build their own churches because the locals accused them of having excessive garlic in their diet which seeped from their

Anything Goes ...

pores and stunk up the building. So, with presumably nowhere for my family to turn, the Levon home became the place of worship. Anyone who lived in or visited my parents' home had to pray upon entering, pray before eating and when finished, and pray again when leaving the home. And because when praying we used the sign of the cross in the name of the Father, the Son, and the Holy Spirit, our true family identity could still be hidden, we could easily hide behind the facade of the Catholic Italian.

I always found it rather contradictory that Father would praise and worship the Lord so faithfully, yet be so money oriented and treat people coldly and callously. When living there I prayed as often as I needed to in order to have access to my home, but deep down my father certainly wasn't the influence on my spirituality. Rather, my faith remained strong through the actions of my mother. She was the epitome of purity and kindness. To me, she truly did represent love. I also, strangely, found a odd sense of spiritual guidance in a cross that lit up the Fresno night. When I was ten years old, I watched the construction of a sixteen-story building in downtown Fresno. It was named the Security Bank Building and was the tallest in the California Central Valley. I remember sitting with my sisters on a sidewalk in downtown Fresno, each of us taking a turn at drinking out of one bottle of Coca-Cola as we watched this building's spectacular grand opening. I saw things that night that I had never seen before. There was a massive spotlight that shone from the street in the dark of night; I thought that maybe the moon had landed. There were fancy cars like the ones in the nickelodeons and movie houses, and many wealthy people. But the most impressive part came later that evening and each night thereafter when the lights in the offices were left on to form a cross on all four sides of the building. It was amazing, and I could see it from anywhere at night in Fresno area. In a child's imagination, I believed that the

Security Bank Building was sent to us by God so that people in Fresno would be reminded that Jesus died for our sins and so that they might not forget to give thanks each night before going to bed. With this in sight and mind, I never forgot to say my childhood prayers.

Despite my sisters' religious upbringing though, and subsequent regular church attendance as adults, some aspects of their personalities had little spiritual content. There was certainly no doubt these ladies had been influenced by the sexual revolution and good-time girls of the 20's, such as the flappers pouring onto the movie screen, and actresses such as the 'IT' girls Clara Bow and Theda Bara, and songs with title's like, 'Anything Goes.' Deep down my siblings were conservative, and somewhat prudish, but just for fun there were times when in the presence of men, they liked to act rather rambunctious and have a good, worldly time. I enjoyed watching their behavior, joining in unless I was too embarrassed, and always got a good laugh.

ONE SUMMER JUNE day, we spent our time together as usual in Elizabeth's front yard. When night drew near, we noticed two men pull up in a jalopy, or struggle buggy as we liked to call it. They parked across the street on the small dirt driveway and began moving some things into the vacant cabin. It was obvious my sisters had noticed them, for their discussion suddenly got louder so as to draw attention our way. And it didn't take long for the men to catch on, finish what they were doing, then cross the street in our direction. As they approached the fence surrounding Elizabeth's yard, I decided to do as I normally would, just observe things as they transpired. I delighted in watching this type of interaction among my sisters and men. I loved to hear the stories that would be told from

both sides and to see in what way my sisters' games or uppity behavior would reject the men.

The men introduced themselves as brothers with the last name
Smith, one named George and the other Lloyd (who preferred to be
called Jack). They, with their two sisters, Grace and Betty, had recently moved to California from the dust bowl of Missouri. George
and Jack were both attractive men, tall with broad shoulders, their
brown hair slicked back, brown eyes, and each had a very thick set
of lips. But regardless of their appearance, George and Jack were
drifters looking for employment in Fresno, sick-making to my single
sisters seeking a financially stable man. The interaction turned out
to be rather brief, as my sisters soon found reason for all the girls to
go inside the house.

After that day I saw, George and Jack in passing quite often
whenever I visited Elizabeth's home, and I learned more about each
of them by listening to my sisters gossip. They thought George was
kind of cute but was unemployed, unskilled, and had once been
jailed as a horse thief. Jack was even more handsome, but was unemployed, unskilled, and had offended Ellen with what she called
'macho malarkey'. Worse yet, Jack was twenty-four years old and
already had a failed marriage under his belt. The nation was well
informed of the rising divorce rate, but it was something foreign to
most of us, and indicated someone not committed to the institution
of marriage. My sisters blamed all of the Smith brothers' faults on
their Protestant upbringing. As they gossiped, I never said a word,
just smiled and listened.

One afternoon, a few weeks after our initial introduction to my
sister's new Midwestern neighbors, I was walking toward
Elizabeth's home. Then suddenly, out of nowhere, Jack approached
me from behind. He realized that he startled me and immediately

said, "Oh, I'm sorry Miss Victoria," chuckling a little.

I stopped for a moment, looked at him strangely, and then continued. I said, "I'm impressed. You remembered my name."

"Of course," he responded. "How could I forgot such a beautiful name or such a beautiful woman."

I smiled and continued to look straight ahead.

Jack walked with me the rest of the way. He talked mostly about the work he had found in local mines, then he asked about my interests. I didn't tell him much, just about my art. Then, as I prepared to enter the gate into Elizabeth's yard, I was very polite and pleasant – as I'm sure my sisters had not been – and said, "Jack, it was nice to see you again. Have a nice day."

There was silence as I walked up the pathway, then I heard him anxiously say, "Victoria, can we talk again some time?"

I continued walking, and without turning as I approached the door, I said, "You can call me Vickie." And I went inside.

Of course my sisters had much to say about my encounter with Jack. They watched the whole thing transpire as each had been staring out the front room window. At first they teased me about liking him and made fun of the Jack and Vickie scenario. Veronica began flinging her arms about and spinning around, and said, "Wouldn't it be grand? Mrs. Victoria Smith."

I suppose I was blushing because the laughing and teasing came to a sudden halt, and my sisters' got very serious.

"You know you could never marry him?" said Elizabeth. "He's no good. And he's not orthodox, father will have a fit."

My eighteen-year-old sister, Dalia said, smiling, "There are lotsa guys out there, Vickie."

"Plus, he already tried to court Ellen," added Angelique.

"Oh, well," I said abruptly, "I'm already pregnant with his child.

Anything Goes …

Experts say talking causes it now, you know!"

Elizabeth, aghast at the idea said, "Vickie, you're a nit!"

I just smiled, and everyone continued on with what they were doing.

FROM THAT DAY forth, every time I approached Elizabeth's house, Jack was there, at the same location, sneaking up behind from around the backside of the same tree. I was certain he watched for me. Eventually I was no longer startled, I could feel him approaching and without looking back I would say, "I know you're there" or "Hello Jack."

He would then walk with me, and we talked a little longer each time. Sometimes we stood outside of Elizabeth's gate and talked, with each of my sisters peering anxiously out the window. Eventually we sat on the ground; our conversations lasted for hours. During this time, some of my nieces and nephews would come near us, then run away giggling. Other times my sisters would attempt to coerce me into the house, but I preferred to stay and learn more about this man that I was increasingly finding more interesting.

Jack told me that he grew up on a farm in Missouri, that his mother died when he was young, and his father and stepmother were both very abusive. In all, he had twelve brothers and sisters, of which he and three others had made their way west.

I asked him about his divorce, and he was very straightforward. "I was young and two-timing," he said. "I gambled a lot, and my wife used to complain about my coming home smelling of alcohol and smoke. Then, I brought home a venereal disease and gave it to her. That was bad enough, but then I didn't get treatment right away, and it sterilized me. She was young and wanted to have children, so she left me."

Jack admitted, "I had a problem, but I feel like I've overcome it."

I admired his honesty, and as shocking as the news was to hear, I considered it a very sincere confession. It certainly didn't effect the way I was beginning to feel about him. I was really starting to like Jack, so I decided to share some inside information about myself, and my family. I told him about my parents, our Armenian background, and the tense feelings that I experienced on occasion with my siblings because of it. I also told him about the stories he would probably hear from my sisters about how our parents met to the lies about Armenian relations to our supposed French and Italian family. Coming from an Irish and Cherokee Indian background, Jack didn't understand the logic behind hiding from ones ethnicity, but reflecting on the toffee-nosed ways in which my sister acted, he wasn't surprised either.

After our long talks, Jack would cross the street to his cabin, and I would enter Elizabeth's house. Each time, without fail, my sisters lectured me.

"Vickie, we told Mom and Dad what you're doing." Elizabeth said. "Dad didn't want to hear it and said he would not approve of such a thing."

Angelique then mocked father in a deep voice saying, "A divorced, unemployed, un-Orthodox man. Not for a daughter of mine!"

Dalia walked by and whispered to me, "Yeah, then right after that Mom said, 'I had hoped she'd find a good Armenian man.' That got all of them quiet." Dalia and I both laughed.

I then reminded my sisters that I was a grown woman, and never once did I interfere in their decision about whom to marry. Yes, I had opinions about the men that they chose, but I never demeaned their choices. I smiled and said, "…and despite what you say, I think

Jack's just peachy."

Of course the older sisters then expressed the fact that their age exceeded mine and therefore so did their wisdom.

I realized that it was probably time for me to tell my mother and father about Jack. I'm sure their impression of him was not a good one, having only heard about him from my sisters. I hoped I could invite him over for dinner so they could make the decision themselves.

I approached my parents on one of the weekend days that my entire family was hanging out around the house. I told them that I wanted to introduce them to a young man that I had met. I asked, "Can my friend Jack join us for dinner?"

At first they were both were reluctant, but when neither of them could give me a straight answer, I told them that it was too late to say no, that he'd be over in an hour.

Elizabeth walked behind me and said with a big smile on her face, "It's not going to work, Vickie."

I worried about what I was getting Jack into. On the other hand, I knew he wasn't a wimp, and I was confident he would be able to handle whatever my family tried to dish out.

The scrutiny began upon his entrance. Jack wasn't familiar with the rule of prayer upon entering our house, so he was immediately criticized for his ignorance. Then, staring at him, my father didn't say a word, mother smiled and nodded her head, and my sisters and their husbands greeted him. Then, my brother Peter walked over to Jack, stuck out his hand, and introduced himself. The two men began talking as everyone else carried on with the barbecue and conversing. I was happy to see my brother so welcoming to-ward Jack, and I looked at Elizabeth and smiled as acknowledg-ment of success.

At dinner, all eyes were on Jack and me. There weren't many smiles on their faces, but at the same time, I found it all quite amusing. Funniest to me was the look of disbelief and surprise on Jack's face when Elizabeth brought up the story of my parents' romantic meeting on that ship. Before she had finished, though, Mother bowed her head, and with the sign of the cross whispered an Armenian thanks in the name of the Father, the Son, and the Holy Spirit, so quickly that I thought it had suddenly just become one long word. Mother raised up from the table and left the room, while I nearly choked on my food.

The evening ended with Jack and I walking down the street as I accompanied him part of the way home. It was a typical Fresno summer night, where the sun would disappear but the heat stayed with us. The moon could not be seen and it was completely dark. The voices of laughter nearby were signs of late-night family gatherings. As we prepared to say goodbye to each other Jack pulled me next to him and hugged me. With the exception of holding my hand on occasion, it was the only time I had ever felt him touch me. But hearing his breath, and feeling the sensation of his pounding heart, was one of the most comforting feelings I had ever known.

After a moment Jack pulled back slightly, looked into my eyes and asked if he could kiss me. I didn't know what to say. Of course I wanted to, but it would be my first kiss. I was extremely frightened. Before I could respond though, Jack's lips softly touched mine. My eyes seemed to close instinctually, melting along with the rest of my body in this man's arms. A strange feeling shot through my body and created a euphoria I hoped could last forever. Then I realized that someone might see us so I pushed back, looked around and said, "I have to go home or they'll come looking for me."

As I walked away I glanced back, and Jack was just standing there watching me. Nervously, I smiled and waved.

Anything Goes ...

When I returned home, my brother, my sisters and their families had all gone home, and my parents were unusually quiet. I walked into my father's office and said, "Goodnight."

"Goodnight, Vickie." He replied without looking my way. Then as I turned to leave he said, "No, I don't approve of him."

I was still in a daze, and most certainly had a silly grin on my face from the kiss I had just received, so I didn't dare turn around to look back.

I simply said, "I'm sorry to hear that."

I went into the kitchen to help Mother clean up before heading to bed. As I dried the dishes and she washed, she said, "I can tell that he loves you, Vickie, but he cannot give you the life you deserve. Please think this through."

I remained quiet, and when I finished the last plate I kissed her on the each cheek, and said "Thanks, Mother. Goodnight."

As I walked out of the kitchen, I heard my mother say, "Heavenly Father, please let her find a good Armenian man." In other words she meant, 'Heavenly Father, please take this man's life.'

Mother knew something was developing between Jack and I, and I lay in bed that night wondering what I was going to do with these feelings. I liked him a lot, and I was certain he liked me too. Yet, no one in my family, except maybe my brother, would accept him. On the other hand, this is the same family who had tried to choose my friends my entire life, thinking they knew what was best for me. In my eyes, their opinions were not always respectable ones. My mother's concern was the only one that truly meant anything to me. Should I wait until I meet an Armenian man so my mother would be happy? What if she was right? What if Jack was in love with me? Is a childless marriage what I want for my life? It was quite a dilemma to face.

I looked out of the bedroom window as I had so many times throughout my life, and in the distance, I saw the cross lighting up the sky from the Security Bank Building downtown. A sense of peace came over me as it always had, and I instantly felt that no matter what happened things would work out. Then I prayed.

SUNDAY AFTERNOONS CONTINUED as they had over the previous two-month period, me walking toward Elizabeth's house, Jack approaching from behind, then walking with me. One day, however, in early November, when we arrived at Elizabeth's house, no one was home and there was a note on the door, written, 'Vickie, we met at Angelique's house today. See you there.'

Angelique lived quite a distance from Elizabeth's house, and I didn't drive so it would take a while for me to get there. I considered just turning back and going home, but then Jack offered to take me. "Or…" he said, "…you could just hang out with me for the day."

I thought about it and figured there could be no harm. "Okay. What do you want to do?"

"Well, I don't know. We could go to the park or the movies. Or we could run away and get married."

I started laughing. Then I looked up at Jack, and he wasn't even smiling. "I'm serious, Vickie." he said.

"What?" I asked, still laughing a bit, only somewhat nervously now.

"We could go to Las Vegas. I have a good job and…"

"Are you crazy?" I interrupted. "Besides…" I laughed, "my family hates you."

There was silence for a moment, then Jack said, "I love you Vickie, and I want you to be my wife."

Anything Goes …

I didn't know what to do. I just stood there in shock and looked at him. He looked into my eyes, and it seemed as though he was staring right into my soul. I realized at that moment that I was in love with this man. I felt the excitement within me begin to rise, then I suddenly burst out. "Okay. Let's do it."

Before I knew it, I was standing in front of a Presbyterian Minister in Las Vegas, Nevada. It was November 1936, and I was now Mrs. Lloyd Hartwell Smith.

Blue Moon …

9

THE BEGINNING STAGES OF THE MARRIAGE WERE SOME-
what strained. First, we had to tell my family. They were disappointed in the person I chose, and that it wasn't done in the traditional way of asking my father's permission first, but they also realized it was too late to do anything about it. They hoped for the best
and accepted it. My sisters surprised me with a bridal shower and
my parents, in the typical Armenian tradition, gave us some money
as a dowry. Then, a week later Jack was laid off from his construction job. The dowry money then went quickly, and soon we were
without a home to live in. My brother and his wife, Elena, allowed
us to stay with them until our situation improved. Despite the circumstances though, Jack and I were disgustingly cheerful. He made
some money working odd jobs and tried very hard to make me
happy.

Six months later, our financial state forced Jack to seek work outside of Fresno and soon we were traveling throughout California, Nevada and Arizona as he worked for six months in one place and one month in another. At first, I was a little frightened to leave the comfort of my hometown and the security of my family, but I loved Jack more than anything, and I was married now – I would have to trust that my husband would care for me.

We ended up in Los Angeles where Jack learned to fly small planes and worked as a pilot transporting mentally ill patients between hospitals. We finally had enough money to live comfortably and enjoy ourselves. I was able to return home to visit my family at least once each month, and Jack bought me gifts from all of the places he visited. He used spare money to buy and distribute food for the homeless people living along the riverbanks. Jack was a hardworking man with a kind heart.

Two years into our marriage, the bliss ended. The money began disappearing, and so too did Jack. He would leave for work and not return home for many days. The first time it happened, I was frightened that something might have happened to him. I tried to contact his employer but had no luck. When he finally came home he told me that he'd been sent to a job out of town. I was suspicious but didn't make an issue of it. The second time it happened, he came home smelling of alcohol and smoke. I knew exactly where he had been.

"You've been gambling, haven't you?" I asked.

"Where's my dinner?"

"It's right there on the table. But it's cold. It's been waiting for you since Monday, and so have I."

Jack noticed that I was upset and came over to hug me. He admitted where he'd been and apologized. He asked me to forgive him and told me he would make it up to me. I could barely stand the smell of him, but at the same time I was happy that he was safe. I accepted his apology and let it go.

The following week Jack and I were back in Fresno, both looking for a job. Although the country was beginning to pull out of the depression, jobs were still scarce, and we had little money. I didn't contact my family because I was embarrassed at the situation I was in. But one morning I was downtown inquiring about hired-help when I ran into my sister Elizabeth. I could tell she was upset at seeing me so desperate, and I suppose she knew times were tough because she asked me if I had eaten. I told her that I had not that day, and she gave me $10.00. I then took her to the hotel room to see Jack. I realized later that it probably wasn't a good idea, because as I expected him to be getting ready for a job interview, Elizabeth and I were both surprised to see that he was still in bed. As Elizabeth turned to leave the room, I tried to explain to her that his job prospects were good, but she wouldn't listen. She said, "I have to go and run some errands. I'll talk to you later." She left without turning back to look at me.

I had hoped that Elizabeth might tell someone else in the family that we were in need of some assistance, and I expected we might be getting an offer to stay at someone's home. But I never heard a word from anyone. Maybe Elizabeth never told, or maybe they wanted us to learn a tough lesson. I'm sure they didn't understand that I actually did see that my life was in a balls-up mess, but I was trying to make the best of the situation. Despite my family's opinion of him, Jack was still the man I had fallen in love with, and I couldn't make him different or more than what he was. I could try to keep him clean from gambling, but that was all I could do. He was my husband and I was in it for the long haul.

Blue Moon ...

Jack found construction work in and around the Fresno area, and soon we earned enough money to rent a small, one-room studio at the Ramona Apartments on L St., downtown. It was located in a section of the Armenian community, so my mother came by to see us, but my sisters didn't visit much. Whenever they did, they refused to enter my home. Instead they would send someone in to get me, and we would visit at the front gate. The only time I was able to see my nieces and nephews was when I visited their homes.

THE NEXT SIX months went quite well. Jack worked hard to provide for me, and during his spare time, he helped to coach a group of neighborhood Armenian teenage girls in their softball league. I worked as his assistant, instructing the girls in proper batting techniques. Since we couldn't have children of our own, it helped to fill the enjoyment Jack and I both found in young people. It was one of the best times in our marriage, and we made a lot of new friends. After softball each night, one young girl named Armine Lazarian, and two sisters, Lydia and Lena Avedikian, used to enjoy hanging out with me, so before sending the girls home on the bus I would treat them to a double scoop ice cream from the milk bar downtown.

Just as we were settling into life in Fresno again, Jack heard about a stable, better paying job at a gold mine in Oatman, Arizona. One week later, on our second wedding anniversary, we were moving again. I hated to have to leave my family and my old and new friends in Fresno, but economically this was important for our future.

In Oatman, Jack was happy to be working in an area he was familiar and comfortable with. Unfortunately, though, I wasn't quite as content. I discovered that the living conditions in this small ghost town left a lot to be desired. We lived in a shack that had holes in the walls. A series of these shanties lined a barren hillside. I wrote

"He was such a stinker ... but your grandmother loved him.'

Blue Moon ...

home to my family and humbly informed them that my home was freezing cold in the winter months, and it was rumored that the weather was much hotter than Fresno during the summer. I told them that my days were spent helping the other miners' wives cook for our husbands and all the single men in the town as well. We were together each day, doing nothing but domestic chores and taking care of the few children that were there. The days soon grew very long.

Even when the men were around, Oatman didn't offer much by way of entertainment. The men challenged each other primarily through card games, and occasionally they would end up competing in arm-wrestling or attempting to shimmy up a nearby rock that resembled an elephant tusk. I thought it was all pretty silly, but I have to admit the I was proud to see Jack and another miner prove to be the strongest pair as they effortlessly climbed this rock and placed an American flag at the top. I've been told that the flag is still there today.

A month after we arrived in Oatman, I became very ill. I was vomiting all day, everyday, and the ladies in town were kind enough to take turns caring for me. I wasn't sure if it was something I had eaten, or maybe the water, or a simple sickness. Then, after two more weeks of constant stomach problems, I found out that I wasn't suffering from an illness at all. Rather, God had decided to create a miracle in my life. I was pregnant.

For more than two years I had thought that Jack and I would never have children, and we were both in shock. If fact, neither of us truly believed it at first, but once my stomach began to grow, it couldn't be denied. Over the next few months, no matter what my day brought me, be it boredom, loneliness, homesickness, or nausea, nothing could bring me down from the euphoria of my pregnancy.

Blue Moon ...

122

On August 19, 1939, with the assistance of some of the other wives in Oatman, I gave birth in my small, hole-in-the-wall shack to a beautiful baby boy. I named him Jack Lloyd Smith, in honor of his father, and called him Little Jackie. The moment I saw him, he became a light in my life that I had never known could shine so bright.

I became engrossed in motherhood, and my husband was a wonderful father. He spent his evenings and weekends helping to take care of our son, and obviously loved him very much. Unfortunately though, his support didn't last long. I think Jack began to feel somewhat neglected since he was no longer receiving as much of my attention as he had before, so he found it elsewhere. Jack had become very friendly with a lady named Kim, a wife of one of the miners. I had for some time suspected they might be having an affair, but I didn't say a word. Then, in May of 1940, when Jackie was nine months old, my suspicions were confirmed. I was awakened early one morning by a knock at the door; I opened it to find Kim's husband, Gregory. He stood there, looked at me, and didn't say a word, just handed me the letter. Kim had written that she and Jack had run off together.

I rushed back to the bedroom and found nothing but empty drawers. I looked at my sleeping child and was suddenly stricken with despair. Beginning to cry, I fell back against the wall, and feeling like a baby myself, I covered my face and sank to the floor. Gregory came in and attempted to comfort me, but there was nothing he could do. He was obviously distraught as well.

I spent the next couple of days watching and waiting for my husband to return. With no sign, and slowly running out of money and food, I was forced to begin to sell any belongings of value. After a week, that too would run out, and I was faced with one of the most painful moments of my life. I realized that my husband wasn't

Only Time

coming back, and I was stranded far away from home. I also realized, though, that it was time to dry my eyes and find a way to get to a place where I could get some help. It was time to return home to Fresno.

The journey would not be an easy one with little money and no transportation, but I began to walk early one morning, carrying any belongings that I could on my back and my son in my arms. Slowly, through many days, we made our way across the Mojave Desert, out of Nevada, and into California. Sometimes I walked with others who also had no transportation and on occasion I was given a lift, once by a couple just married in Las Vegas, another by a man returning to California from a gambling spree in Nevada. The last ride was offered by a truckload of men who actually thought that I was pretending to carry a child in order to get a pity-ride from someone. When they pulled over to the side of the road one of them said, "Look, she's trying to act like she's carrying a baby under that blanket."

I just ignored them and kept walking.

They stopped the truck and one of them said, "Hey, lady, wait."

He ran up to me so I stopped and just looked at him. As he slowly peeked under the blanket that shielded Little Jackie from the sun, he asked, "Do you and..."

He looked back at his friends and said, "Hey, she does have a baby under here."

"Where are you headed?"

"I'm going to Fresno."

"Well, come on, we'll give you a ride."

He and another man hopped into the back of the truck, allowing Little Jackie and me to ride in the front. They took us all the way to my parents' doorstep. Five days after leaving Oatman, Arizona, I was finally home.

Blue Moon ...

LIFE BACK IN Fresno was bittersweet. I was happy to be in a comfortable place where my family could finally get to know Little Jackie, but on the other hand I was embarrassed that I was returning under such shameful conditions. My family was constantly there to remind me of my mistakes with the 'I told you so,' and the 'you should have known better.'

Basic Jack bashing went on for quite some time and I dealt with it the best way I knew how, which was to just let them say whatever they needed to. At times I even began to believe some of what I was hearing, questioning my own judgement and feeling regret. But then each time I saw my son laughing as he played with his cousins or lay cradled in his grandmother's arms, I wondered how the marriage could have been so wrong when it produced someone so wonderful. Little Jackie truly was a miracle child.

It took some time to adjust to my new life. I had to build the strength to explain to family and friends why I was home with a child, yet without a husband. I was never one that was too concerned with others' opinions, but this was an emotional time for me, which made it more difficult. In the end, it was Little Jackie that got me through it. I dealt just fine with the whispering behind my back and negative perception some people had. There was no time to be weak. I had to be strong for my son.

Six months after my return I was still living at home with my parents. I reestablished some ties with my family and friends, and I worked as a clerk at Long's Drug Store in downtown Fresno. At the time it was unusual for a woman to be employed outside of the home, but still I found it enjoyable. It also seemed to give the busybodies something else to talk about other than my failed marriage; now they questioned my parenting. But even that didn't bother me; I knew my son was in the wonderful care of my mother, and she was in absolute heaven.

Only Time

Wait

"But Vickie loved her son very much. Little Jackie was her life. She treated him like a king."

At home, my father continued to make life difficult. He hated Jack for what he had done, and I heard about it every day. He made comments quite frequently about how Little Jackie resembled his father, and how no man would ever want me now; I would be alone forever. Occasionally when my sisters were visiting, they would join in and talk about how my poor my decision was to marry Jack. They then began to tie it in to the friends that I had chosen. One said, "The same thing is going to happen if you continue your friend-ships with Armenians."

But I was not going to allow my sisters' scare tactics to dictate my choice in friends, not when their reasoning was based on preju-dice and fears of exposure. I remained silent, though; arguing with them would have only made matters worse.

One afternoon when I returned home from work, my father began his usual lecture. I did as I had done before and let him talk. He recited scripture to me and professed morals and responsibility. Occasionally I would politely correct him or try to explain my point of view, but as always it did no good. This time, though, things ended differently. He left the room where my mother and I were sitting, then came back in and said, "I no longer want that man's son living in my home. I am not going to support a child that be-longs to such a sinful man. You can live here..." He said, "...but not the boy. And your mother is no longer allowed to care for him." And he walked out.

Immediately I looked at my mother, sitting in her rocking chair. She just shook her head and closed her eyes. We both knew there was nothing either of us could do, and I broke into tears. I relied on my parents for a home and for childcare. I worked, so I could prob-ably afford a place of my own, but who would care for Little Jackie? People didn't just open their homes to children of working moth-ers.

Blue Moon ...

I asked my sisters for help, but each claimed to already have too much responsibility; they really couldn't take on caring for another child. I contacted some of my girlfriends, and between three of them, they were able to watch Jackie when I worked during the day. I also picked up a second job as a waitress at a Chinese food restaurant in the evenings. I moved out of my parents' house and into the Ramona Apartments where Jack and I had lived a couple of years before. I contacted Armine and Lena and Lydia, the young Armenian girls we used to coach in softball and each was able to assist in caring for Little Jackie in the afternoon and evening.

This arrangement was difficult, but worked for a while, until, that is, the United States entered WWII. Many husbands were sent to war, and their wives were either financially forced or encouraged to join me in the ranks of those women working outside of the home. I suddenly lost my primary childcare options as my girlfriends now worked by my side.

I had to figure out what I was going to do. I refused to resort to the measures chosen by other working mothers, leaving their children in locked cars during their shift and checking on them during break time. Others let their children roam the city and attend movies all day. I had a two-year old son and was going to make sure he was cared for. I just didn't know how that was going to happen.

I wished I could look out of my window at night as I prayed and find the peace that used to consume me whenever I saw the cross on the side of the Security Bank Building. But rising electricity costs caused the need for a cutback in expenses, so the lights were no longer left on at night in the building offices. Instead, I prayed without it, and I asked God to please help me find a way through this.

One afternoon as I was preparing for work, Lena and Lydia came over to baby-sit. Arriving with them were their parents, Mary and

Al. Al said, "The girls told us about your predicament Vickie. You know, Mary and I have boarded children before. We understand that your situation is only temporary, and we'd love to take Jackie into our home until you can pull things together."

I was surprised at such an offer, especially since it was an idea that had never even crossed my mind. It almost seemed too absurd to even think about.

I kindly thanked Al and Mary for their concern, but could not accept, "Because..." I said, "...I could never place my child in another person's home. I can't imagine not having Little Jackie to come home to each night."

They paused for a moment, looked at each other, then Mary said, "At least think it over. If you change your mind, we'll contact welfare services and help you through the process."

I went to work that night scared to death. The thought of not raising my child caused fear to rush through me. On the other hand, not being able to provide for him while I worked, or not working and having no home or food for him, frightened me also.

I cried a lot and continued to pray. I also went to my mother for advice and was shocked at her response.

"Take him to their home." She said.

"What?"

"He'll be cared for by Armenians..." she said, "...and there is nothing better. Vickie, no other child in our family has the opportunity to live as an Armenian, but now Little Jackie has that chance."

With disappointment in her voice she said, "He might be the saving Grace in all the lies that surround us."

Then she turned to me and said, "Other than you or I taking care of him, I can't think of anything that would make me happier.

Vickie, take him to the Avedikian home. It is best for now."

This was such a difficult decision, and not only because of my own selfish concerns as a parent who didn't want to lose her child. I was also afraid my sisters might treat Jackie differently if I placed him in an Armenian home. I hadn't yet told my son of his Armenian heritage; I was planning to wait until he was old enough to understand why his relatives denied such a thing and why they preferred to hide it. He already unknowingly paid the price for the mistakes of his father, and if I placed him in this home, my family might further distance themselves from him. As I contemplated this decision, I began to think of Little Jackie's immediate well-being above my own, and above the concerns of my family. I was confident that he would be well cared for in the Avedikian home, and being somewhat familiar with hearing my mother speak the language and cook the food, I knew he would adapt well with the Armenian culture that would surround him every day.

I showed up on the Avedikian's doorstep in tears two days after their offer. I said, "You have to know that this is only temporary. And I have to be able to see him as much as I want."

Both Mary and Al assured me that I would be allowed in their home at any time, and that Little Jackie would have the best care he could receive with a complete family, both parents, plus Lena, Lydia, their sister Lucy, and their brother, Kerry, to take care of him.

I was just a mess the day I sat down and discussed arrangements with the welfare worker at the Avedikian's home. As my son slept in a nearby room, we decided that I would pay social services $20.00 each month, visit Jackie every weekend, and take him overnight when I wanted. It was all I could do not to cry as I sat in this home discussing when and where I would be seeing my son.

While I was there, Lena and Lydia came running in the house from school, asking excitedly, "Is he here?"

Only Time

"Yes," Mary responded, "but don't wake him; he's taking a nap."

The girls stood very still, and looked at us for a moment while glancing over at Jackie's bedroom door. I looked at Mary and Al, stood up, walked over to the bedroom door, smiled at the girls, and opened it for them. Lena and Lydia burst into the room where Little Jackie lay there sucking his thumb. Tears filled my eyes when he looked up at the girls, pulled his thumb out of his mouth, smiled, and reached out for them. I found some immediate comfort with the decision I was making.

Leaving the Avedikian home that day was one of the hardest things I'd ever done. I waited until Jackie's attention was focused on Lena and Lydia, and I sneaked out of the back door. I collapsed in tears on the porch. I looked at the sky and cried, then bowed my head and prayed, "God, please help me to get my son back."

I MADE A pact with myself that day that I would be with Little Jackie every single weekend, and I never broke that promise. I picked up a third job during the week as a clerk at the local Army Depot, Hammer's Field Post Exchange. My weekends were devoted to my son. Each Saturday morning I caught a bus that took me within two blocks of the Avedikian home. And it never failed, as I walked off of the bus and down the street, my son stood on the front porch waiting for me. Most of the time, Lena, Lydia, and their older sister, Lucy, stood with him. I would always see him peering down the street in my direction, and when he saw me approaching, he jumped up and down, pointing and yelling. I couldn't understand exactly what was being said, but I did hear the word 'Mommy,' the only word that truly mattered.

It was such a feeling of elation, the times we spent together walking through a park, swimming at the local pool, or just hanging out at the Avedikian home. My weekends were healing to any despair I felt about losing my son. Also, considering he was now a welfare child, I realized how lucky I was to be able to take him to spend entire weekends at my parents' home or one of my sisters' homes. I couldn't care for Little Jackie on my own, but there was a wonderful family that took over for what I could not provide, and yet still allowed me to give my son whatever I could give.

On the other hand, whereas Saturday mornings were joyful, Sunday afternoons were not. I had to return my son to the Avedikian's home, and I became very sad. I wondered why the situation had to be this way. Why couldn't I have a family like my sisters? Why couldn't I have a responsible husband to care for my child and me? At times I felt angry with my husband for breaking his promise to love and provide for me forever, and I was also angry with my family for not helping. Sunday nights alone in my apartment were the worst of times.

Each workweek, I began by telling myself that I was actually working toward a goal, and I would eventually be able to provide for my son again. Most of my spare money went into savings. In fact, I took Jackie to the banker once and told him, "If anything ever happens to me, remember this man and remember this place."

Of course, however, I did spend some of my extra money shopping. For myself I purchased a gold signet ring with Jackie's initials engraved across the top, as well as the expense of semi-annual portraits of Jackie and I. These are things that I felt kept my son near to me when we had to be apart. For Jackie, I bought anything he wanted that I considered practical. I gave him clothes, a pair of boots that he begged me for and wore every day after, and roller-skates that he assured me he could use without falling – only later regretting it as I watched him fall all over the street learning to skate.

*"My foster parents were Mary and
Al, and they had four teen-age
children of their own."*

Blue Moon ...

*"I remember when
mom bought those
(boots) for me."*

*"Mom used to lick her
finger, then twist it through
my hair to make that ringlet
over my ear."*

Blue Moon …

One year passed, and another, then another. I had no idea how long this situation would last. During my times of desperation I hoped my husband would return to me so I could have a family life again. Other times I considered divorcing him and marrying another. Occasionally on a Friday night some of my Armenian girlfriends would drag me out to a ballroom dance club called the 'The Rainbow Room.' I met a few very nice men there, and in fact, I dated on occasion. But nothing ever came of those men; most were interested in a sexual relationship, and I wasn't.

Outside of those encounters, however, I did fall in love at one point, and considered marriage to another. First, there was Demitri, a Greek serviceman from New York. I met him when he was stationed in Fresno at the Hammer's Field Post Exchange Army Depot. We dated for just over a year and got along wonderfully. Demitri and I were the same age, ate the same types of food, and in general had a lot in common. The Greeks and Armenians had many similarities in their cultures, and for centuries had experienced the same historical persecution by Turks. It was the first time I'd ever felt comfortable being Armenian around someone who was not. Also, the year was 1943 and Demitri and I shared in reliving the pain of what the Turks had done to the Greeks and Armenians during WWI by watching the events of the post-WWII exposure of the Jewish Holocaust. It was disturbing to hear and read accounts of the Jews having to suffer at the hands of Adolf Hitler as the Greeks and Armenians had to endure by the Turks only twenty-five years before. Particularly disturbing about it all was that in all the years since the WWI, Armenians had struggled to bring recognition to what was referred as the 'Forgotten Genocide' in order to prevent history from repeating itself. Unfortunately, their efforts appeared to be in vain when it was reported that Adolf Hitler was quoted as saying in his preparation of invading Poland, "Besides, who remembers the Armenians?" And the saddest part about that is that it was true; few remembered. But the Greeks and Armenians could never forget, and as predicted, history did repeat itself. Demitri and I always believed that the second Holocaust of modern times could have possibly been prevented had the world chosen to remember the first one that occurred.

But, with regard to my relationship, as it is said, 'all good things must end'. Demitri made it clear from the beginning that he didn't want to marry someone who already had a child, and after the war, he left Fresno. It was a difficult time for me because I loved him very much. But I cried only at having to lose my best friend, not because he didn't want to marry me. I stood firm on the fact that my son was my life, and any man who wanted to be with me for more than a friendship would have to accept us both.

The next man I dated somewhat seriously was very friendly, one of the nicest I'd ever known. His name was Jeffery, but everyone called him Red because his face turned bright whenever he laughed. He loved Jackie and me and wanted to marry me. But I was still legally married, had not yet decided if I wanted to declare Lloyd deceased, and I refused to file for divorce. I had made a promise to God that I would remain married to Jack through thick and thin, even if Jack failed to hold up on his end of the deal. Red told me that he could not wait, all with the uncertainty of Jack's possible return, so we parted. In the end, I believe it was probably best anyway, for I really wasn't physically attracted to Red nor was I in love with him, and I feared that I might be considering marriage to him only for the ability to raise my son.

Loneliness was difficult, and at times, it took all I had not to search for him and file those divorce papers, accept the first offer of marriage I received, and have my child with me again. But, marriage was sacred to me. So despite my occasional bouts with depression, I continued to live my weekdays at work, and my weekends with my son. Those two simple days each week were truly the best times of my life. We were buddies, and hung out like friends, but I was still a mother. I used to panic at the local swimming pool when Jackie would jump into the deep end and unable to swim; he sat at the bottom certain that someone would dive in to get him. I don't know if it was the fear of his drowning or the shrill in my voice as I yelled him name, but someone always followed him in and pulled him back to the surface. I also enjoyed taking him to the movie house. My favorite part was intermission when the big band would play. I always stood up and requested "Blue Moon." It was my favorite song because it reminded me of how my life had been changed with the birth of my son. My moon had been turned from blue to gold.

IN JANUARY OF 1949, I had been a single mother for almost nine years, living apart from my son for eight. But I was still optimistic that something would turn around. For the time being, however, I was comforted by the care the Avedikians were giving to Little Jackie, and they had grown to love him very much. Al once sat me down and told me that he loved my son as his own. He asked if he could adopt him. I had to tell him that there was absolutely no way; I could never do it. As grateful as I was to them, I couldn't give my son away. I told Al that I loved Jackie more than anything, and that I really wanted to have him in my life. I assured him that things would change, and I would be able to provide for my son again one day.

I had no idea exactly how that change would occur, but it finally began only one month after my conversation with Al. I was still working at the drugstore during part of my day, when one morning I noticed a customer walk in the store. He was a tall, handsome man who looked very familiar. I noticed him glancing around the store so I turned away, not wanting him to catch me staring, and I focused my attention back toward the items I was stocking on the shelves. I could see this man in my peripheral vision as he walked down the isle towards me, and as he approached I began to feel a very strange sense of emptiness in my stomach. This man then stopped directly beside me, and said, "Hello, Vickie."

My breath came to a halt. I immediately knew who it was. My husband had returned. It took a moment for me to respond, as I stared straight ahead then closed my eyes. I then took a deep breath and turned slowly toward him, but I couldn't speak a word. I had always wondered what I would say if I ever saw Jack again. Now the moment had arrived, and all I could do was turn away and continue what I was doing.

"How are you?" he asked.

"Is there something I can help you find, sir?"

"Can we talk?"

"I have work to do," I abruptly replied.

As I walked away, each step seemed to last forever. I could hear my heart beating a thousand times a minute, and all noise seemed to be muffled. When I reached the end of the aisle, I turned around to see if he was following me, but he was not. Jack was gone.

I thought about my husband a lot after that encounter. Each day I worked I watched the door as the customers entered. In a way, I was hoping he would come back, yet fearing it at the same time. I had so many mixed emotions I really didn't know what I felt toward him after all these years. There was definitely some anger, some resentment, and some hatred. But I worried about him, wondered where he had been, why he left, and why he was now returning after all this time. Maybe he was back to reconcile, maybe back to divorce me. The time had now come for me to seriously think about what I was going to do with my marriage.

I also thought about how my son might react to his father's return. I told him about Jack when he was three years old. I showed him pictures and explained to him that his father lived far away. But I worried that if I were to let Jackie see him now, it might affect him if Jack were to disappear again. I would never want my child to experience the pain of abandonment as I had, and it was my responsibility as a parent to protect him. I would have to be very careful in my decision making.

One week after his initial visit to the store, Jack returned. This time he carried a dozen roses and a box of candy. He walked straight up to me as I was working the cash register, and said, "Please talk to me, Vickie."

I was uncomfortable as everyone in the store had their eyes glued on my next move, so I took the vase and the box, set them on the counter, and said, "Meet me at the Courthouse Park in thirty minutes."

It seemed like the longest half-hour of my life. My mind was so busy trying to figure out what I was going to do and say, I couldn't even concentrate on my duties. After my shift I walked over to the Courthouse Park, and there on the bench sat my husband. It was difficult for me to look him in the eyes, so I approached, sat down, looked straight ahead, and said, "Go ahead and talk."

"Well..." he said. "I spent a lot of my time in the Philippines working on runways during the war. Then my brother George, his wife Lillian, and I worked in Washington State picking potatoes for a while. We slowly made our way down to California. I sent letters to your parents' home, but never got a response."

"I never received any letters."

"Vickie..." he said as he turned towards me, "I've wanted to come and find you so many times, but as each year past, it got harder." The was a brief moment of silence, and he asked, "How's my son?"

"My son is beautiful." I replied as I continued to look straight ahead. "He's a wonderful little boy, and still as much the light of my life as he was when I carried him through the desert after his father ran off with some floozy. I couldn't afford to care for him on my own so now he's boarded."

Jack was silent. He then knelt down in front of me, and said, "Please look at me."

I tried, but I just couldn't, especially since my eyes were beginning to fill with tears.

"I am so sorry." He said. "I'm sorry for everything I've put you through."

Oddly enough, those simple words alone took an immediate weight off of my heavy heart. I realized that all I wanted to hear was a sincere apology. I suddenly felt a strange sense of relief. I was finally able to look into his eyes, and I said, "Thank-you."

Then I got up and said, "I have to go. I have a job I have to get ready for. I'll see you sometime, Jack." And I left.

After that I didn't worry too much about seeing Jack again. The thought of him didn't bother me, and my mind wasn't consumed with him at all. I was at ease with his return, and I had no expectations of him or myself. I chose not to tell Little Jackie about my meeting with his father. I decided to wait, and if Jack planned on staying around for while, maybe then I would allow him access to his son.

JACK STAYED IN Fresno. He worked in construction and visited my store on occasion. At first we were cordial towards each other, and we gradually became friends again. All the while, Jack constantly asked me if he could see his son, but I refused. I wasn't yet comfortable with the idea. Finally, a couple of months later, I decided it was time to reunite father and son.

It was a Saturday morning in March of 1949. I invited Jack to my home, and had him wait there while I rode the bus to pick up Little Jackie. The scene that morning was as it had always been. The bus dropped me off, I walked toward the Avedikian home, and as I approached, there stood my son watching for me. Then, when in his sight, I could see him jump up and down and scream, "…. Mommy." It brought tears to my eyes every time. This time, however, as I walked closer to him the tears began to swell, and I started to cry. This weekend was not going to be like the others, and I wasn't sure what impact it would have on him. I prayed to God that I was making the right decision.

Jackie and I rode the bus into the city instead of out toward my parents' house as we ordinarily did first thing Saturday morning.

He asked, "Mommy, aren't we going to visit Grandma Anna?"

"No, not today."

"Are we going to visit Aunt Elizabeth?"

"No."

"Aunt Angelique?" he asked.

Jackie loved to visit our relatives. At my parents' house, my mother greeted him with a big hug and a bowl of shredded wheat cereal. At my sisters' homes, he enjoyed playing with all of his cousins. Elizabeth's youngest daughter, three-year old Linda, was one of his favorites. She was the only cousin he had known since the time of her birth, and I think he also had an attachment to her because she looked a lot like his Grandma Anna. I used to tease Elizabeth about Linda looking so Armenian, and I once asked her, "Elizabeth, what are you going to do, tell people that it's caused from

144

those darned Armenians marrying into our family? Just tell them, 'You see what that intermarriage does, we all start looking Armenian!" Mother and I laughed. Elizabeth didn't respond.

Jackie also liked to watch the adults play like children as well. The weekend Angelique's husband, Les, took me for a ride on his motorcycle, I was so scared that I screamed all way down the street. Jackie and Angelique's son, Frank, stood in the front yard laughing hysterically.

But I said, "No, Jackie. I have something at my apartment that I want to show you. But it's a surprise, so you can't ask me questions about it. Okay?"

Excitedly, he said, "Okay," smiling and placing his index finger in front of his lips as an indicator of silence.

I couldn't help but smile in adoration of him, he had such a strong spirit, and was so happy. God had truly blessed me with an amazing child. He was full of innocence, truth, and goodness. I stared out of the window and prayed that he could endure any outcome this meeting might bring.

When Jackie and I entered my apartment, Lloyd stood up from the couch. I knelt beside my son and said, "Jackie, remember when I told you that you're father lived far away?"

"Yes." he said, his stare glued upon Jack.

"Well, he has moved to Fresno. Jackie this is your father."

The smile of a very shy, yet excited child came upon Jackie's face. Still looking at Jackie he quietly said, "Hello."

Jack walked forward and knelt down in front of Jackie. He said, "I haven't seen you since you were a baby. I've missed you, son."

Jack then held out his arms and said, "May I have a hug?"

Little Jackie grinned and as I fought back tears, my son leapt into his father's arms.

The three of us spent much of that weekend together. Jack stayed with Jackie and I until Saturday evening, then met us for breakfast Sunday morning and a afternoon picnic in the park.

Later that evening I took Jackie back to the Avedikians. When we walked into the house, Jackie ran up to Al and hopped in his lap, as he did every weekend, and said, "I have two dads and two moms."

"Okay." Al replied, looking at the others curiously.

"I met my other dad!" said Jackie.

"You did?" Al replied looking at me even more curious.

"Yes," I interrupted, "Jack moved back to Fresno a few months ago."

"Oh," said Al. He then looked at Mary and his daughters, who all had an expression of concern on their faces. With tears filling his eyes and a forced smile on his face, Al said, "That's wonderful, Jackie. You're a lucky boy."

Al motioned to have Lena and Lydia take Jackie to the other room, which they did by asking Jackie to tell them all about his weekend. Then, obviously fighting back tears, his voice choking a bit, Al asked, "Are you and Jack going to take him from us?"

I took a deep breath and said, "Al, I don't know what's going to happen. I've thought a lot about it, and I'm really not sure what I'm going to do. Jack has asked me on several occasions to considering taking him back, but I never respond. I'm in a tough situation here. I want more than anything to have my family together again, and working now is much harder than it was during the war. Most of the other women have gone home to take care of their kids. I'm either going to have to just get it over with and divorce my husband or return to him. But whatever happens, please know that I love all of you for everything that you've done, and I'll certainly let you know as soon as I decide."

Blue Moon ...

Al was quiet as the tears rolled down his cheeks. Mary spoke up and said, "You know we love this boy, Vickie."

"I know." I said.

JACK CONTINUED TO visit Jackie and me on the weekends. Occasionally I left them alone so they could spend time together. But when I was there, I watched every move Jack made, scoring each of his actions as though he was being unknowingly tested in his abilities as a father and as a mate. He was passing with flying colors. We were all having a wonderful time together.

Another month passed, I still had not made a decision regarding my marriage, but then I found myself faced with a sudden sense of urgency. Mary Avedikian had become ill and required immediate surgery. With no one else in the home capable of caring for my son, Welfare Services told me that he would have to be moved to another boarder. It was then that I decided to return to my husband. I believed that life with Jack would benefit Jackie much more than being placed in a new home full of strangers to us both. Some considered it risky, but it was a chance I had to take for the well being of my son.

I knew this transition would not be an easy one. First of all, the Avedikian family was distraught. They worried about Mary possibly not surviving the surgery, and they cried at having to lose Little Jackie. And although Jackie was excited about living with Jack and me, the separation was tough on him, too. Jackie loved this family very much.

Then came the issue of telling my family. I knew for certain that they would not approve. Dad's first words were, "You need to let your son go to anyone willing to take him before relying on that man again."

Only Time

I tried to explain the situation to him, but his mind was very narrow. I said, "You just don't understand."

"You're making a mistake," he said. "He'll just leave you again."

"I have no choice here. Father, I'm not an idiot. Of course I realize he could leave again, but at least I have to give it a try. And in case things don't work out, I'd like you to hold some money for me. I have $3000 in a Savings Account, and as my husband, Jack will always have access to it. But, if you have it, he can't touch it. This way I'll always know it's there in case I need it."

Father just shook his head in disgust, and said, "Fine, but I don't think it's a good idea."

Mother was sitting in a nearby room listening to the conversation between my Father and me, and as I walked by her to leave she said, "You know, Vickie, you can mend a broken jar but you can never erase the cracks."

She too was concerned about this decision I was making. I stopped, turned toward her, walked over and gave her a kiss on each cheek, and said, "I'll be fine."

Within a week, Jack and Jackie moved in with me and my life changed drastically. I now stayed at home during the day, sent my son off to school, and drew my pictures of the Armenian landscape. I was home when Little Jackie returned, helped him with his homework, and cooked dinner every night. I missed the social aspects of working outside of the home, but I was also happy and content as a housewife.

And as he had been in the first few months of Jackie's life, Jack was a wonderful husband and father. He wanted to provide for his family, so much so that he sought and was given a promotion at work. It was higher pay and more consistent hours, but it also required us to move to Los Angeles. I hated to leave my family and friends again, and all that I had worked for in Fresno, but my husband and son had to come first.

In Los Angeles, all of Jack's spare time was spent with Jackie and me. On weekends we would picnic or take Jackie to play at a nearby park. Occasionally we would all go to a local beach where Jackie and I would wait while Jack chartered a plane and flew aerial acrobatics above our heads. Jackie used to get so excited at all of us being together, and it gave me such a sense of joy having him with me and seeing him so happy. Plus, although I could not forget the past, I was also falling in love with Jack all over again.

It was May of 1949, and everything was wonderful in my life. My husband, my son and I were finally back together. Unfortunately though, it seemed I could not have my happiness and please everyone else as well. My family had distanced themselves further since I had returned to Jack. I wrote to them, but my sisters' never wrote back. Mother was the only one to respond; she herself going through some turbulent times at home.

She told me that Father had received a postcard regarding some Negroes he had sold property to. The postcard was supposedly sent from the Ku Klux Klan and attempted to scare my father into forcing the Negroes off the land and out of the neighborhood. After Father showed the postcard to a neighbor, the FBI was contacted. They began an investigation and in the end accused my father of writing the postcard himself, in an attempt to retrieve land that he had sold to the Negroes. Mother had no idea if Father was guilty of the crime, but said he was taken to the police department because his handwriting was similar to that on the postcard. There he was forced to submit a handwriting sample of the alleged threats, during which he misspelled the word neighborhood, writing 'neighbourhood,' exactly as it had been misspelled on the postcard. Father was initially charged with extortion and spent some time in County Jail, but after further investigation the local District Attorney decided to drop the charges, as did the FBI.

Mother also wrote of other distressing news. She told me that although Mary Avedikian had recovered fully from her surgery, Al died soon thereafter from heart failure. It was rumored that he died of a broken heart from missing a young boy who had been in care at his home. This news was very upsetting to me, and in a strange way, I felt somewhat responsible. I cried for days, wanting to return to Fresno and pay my last respects, but at the same time I didn't want to tell Little Jackie that his 'other Dad' had passed away. Instead, I sent the Avedikians a card with recent pictures of Jackie, and decided to keep the news to myself and not upset my son.

In July I was growing more content with an emotionally and financially stable husband, I started to notice a change in Jack. He began coming home late, and as in the years before, smelled of smoke and alcohol. Instant fear shot through me. It was a very strange feeling, as though I'd never been so frightened in my life. I begged Jack not to return to that lifestyle, and he assured me that everything would be fine.

One day Jack didn't return home from work. In fact, for five days I waited, but nothing. During this time I cried, but tried not to let anyone notice. I carried on as normally as possible, getting my son ready for school, helping him with his homework, cooking dinner, and playing with him at the park. When he asked about his father, I told him that he was away at work.

When Lloyd finally did come home, something unusual happened. I can't really say exactly what it was because I don't remember it. All I know is that when I saw him my heart began to race, and I had difficulty catching my breath. The next thing I knew I was lying on my back on the bed, Little Jackie and our neighbor were standing at the doorway, and Jack was straddling my body and restraining my arms, sternly repeating, "Vickie, calm down."

Blue Moon ...

150

Jack told me later that I had attacked him, and he'd been holding me down for nearly two hours. I didn't know how to respond to this; I had no idea of how or why it happened. I apologized to Jack and just hoped it would never happen again.

Jack came home pretty consistently each night after that, for about a week or so, but then it happened again. He didn't return from work one day; he didn't come home the next day, or the next. I was frightened, and I cried again but tried not to let my son see me upset. The third night without any contact from my husband, I remember preparing dinner as usual, and as I was stirring soup, Jackie swayed back and forth in the kitchen entryway – singing. I felt my heart begin to race, and again I had trouble catching my breath. The next thing I knew I was in the bedroom standing over my son with a pan gripped in my hand and raised up over my head preparing to strike. Jackie was balled up into a fetal position, leaning against the wall and screaming "Stop, Mommy. Stop!"

I realized what I was doing and dropped the pan, grabbed my son, and held him in my arms. As I began to cry, I said, "Oh, my goodness, Jackie, Mommy's so sorry."

I held my son for as long as I could that night. I lay with him in bed, sleepless out of concern for my marriage, my son, and now myself. I worried about what was happening to me.

The following day Jack came home. This time he admitted he'd been gambling again, but this time he missed so much work that he'd lost his job. He told me that we were going to have to move north to Sacramento, near his brother George and George's wife Lillian, where a job had been lined up for him.

I didn't want to go to Sacramento, and I didn't want to stay in Los Angeles either. I didn't know what I wanted anymore. But I saw that Jackie was excited about living near his cousin, George and Lillian's daughter Dorothy. He could play with her as he had

"We started living as a family again and things seemed fine at first. I could tell that Mom was happy."

done so often with my sisters' children in Fresno, I had to agree to go. I tried to remain happy and sane for the sake of my son, wearing a smile, but inside I was very upset. What could I do, though? Go back to Fresno to a family who wouldn't help? Hand my son over to welfare again, to a stranger's home, and divorce my husband? I didn't want to lose my son again, and to keep him, I was stuck.

In Sacramento, we lived in an apartment across the street from where George and Lillian rented one of a series of train cars that had been converted into a home. George and Jack worked together driving a cab while Lillian and I stayed home with our children.

Things were okay at first, with Jack drinking only on occasion, and at least he was coming home on a regular basis. Before long, though, he started gambling again and rarely returned home from work. When he did come home, he was broke, claiming he'd been robbed. Slowly we ran out of money and food, and then our clothes and household items began to disappear. Jack even sold some of my drawings and paintings to pay for his habit, and when he had nothing else to sell, he came to me. He said, "You know, my sisters both work at a whorehouse in the San Francisco Bay Area. We could make a lot of money if you worked there, too."

I was so disgusted with him at this point in our marriage I wasn't even surprised. I just said, "You're crazy!"

"Well then if we can't afford to take care of our son…" he said, "he might have to be boarded out again." He was trying his best to coerce me through fear.

"It's not going to work, Jack."

I tried not to let him notice but I truly was terrified. If my husband could reach a point where he would suggest that I work in a whorehouse to feed his gambling debts, things were even worse than I imagined. I had no idea what this man was capable of, and I feared he might do something drastic. Would he offer to sell my son next? All I could do was watch Jackie closely and pray that the situation would get better.

IN EARLY DECEMBER, Jack was not home, and evening was progressing. Our electricity had been shut off, so I went out to chop wood for a fire. I knew that Jackie was out taking his puppy for a walk, and I realized that he should have returned home by this point. I got very concerned that something might have happened, and I decided to go and look for him. I walked around the neighborhood calling out his name, but got no response. I asked, but no one had seen him. I felt anxiety and panic build within me as I ran around screaming out his name. I was certain that my husband had followed through on my worst fears and had taken him. As I headed for Lillian's house to see if Jackie might be there, I felt my heart begin to race, and as before, I began to gasp for air, having difficulty catching my breath.

The next thing I knew I was inside my apartment, sitting in a chair being restrained by police officers. There was one on each side, one at my shoulders, and one holding my feet. I didn't know what had happened, but something must have. I had no recollection of returning home or anything leading up to this situation. Jack was home now, standing near me, and Lillian was talking to a police officer. I heard her tell him that I had come looking for Jackie with an axe in my hand and blank stare in my eyes. She said Jack had warned her that I might act strangely, and to call him if something happened.

She said, "I told Vickie that I had not seen Jackie. Then, when I watched Vickie walk towards her home, I went to the school nearby, found Jackie, and told him that his mother was acting strange and that he should go and hide. I called Jack at work, and he told me to call the police."

Still in somewhat of a daze I said, "I was cutting wood. We don't have any heat." When no one responded I asked one of the police officers, "Why are you holding my ankles so tightly? It hurts."

"Because..." he said, "...the officer holding your shoulders has a shoe print on his face, and since you can't keep your feet on the ground, I'll have to help you."

I said, "Please tell me what's going on."

Just then I saw my son appear at the front door with his puppy in his arms. I didn't know what to say to him, and I hated for him to have to see this.

One of the policemen said, "Stand up, Mrs. Smith."

Still dazed and confused, I didn't comply immediately. I just looked at him curiously.

"I said stand up, Mrs. Smith." he said, and I was pulled out of the chair.

My hands were forced behind my back and locked into handcuffs, and I was led out of the apartment.

As I passed my son, I was crushed inside from the sadness and the concerned look on his face. I said, "I'm sorry Jackie. You know I love you."

As I was escorted down the walkway in front of all of my neighbors, I saw the police car that awaited me. It was then that I realized I was actually being taken away.

I told the policemen, "Wait. I want to give something to my son."

Then, with my hands cuffed behind my back, I removed from my finger the ring that had Jackie's initials engraved on it, allowing it to drop to the ground. I turned and faced my son, still standing in the doorway watching me, and I knelt to the ground. As Jackie walked towards me, I said, "Jackie, Mommy's so sorry." I started to cry.

Blue Moon ...

I looked down at the ring on the ground and said, "When you were younger, this is all I ever had to keep you near me when we were apart. Whenever I missed you, all I had to do was look at it, and I felt as though you were right there with me. Now I don't know where I'm going or how long I'm going to be there, so I'm giving it to you. When you miss me, all you have to do is look at this ring, and you'll know I'm there with you."

Jackie placed his dog on the ground and picked up the ring. I could see in his eyes that he felt sorry for me. Jackie knew that I was a good person, but there was just something wrong. He reached out and hugged me, and with tears beginning to stream down his cheeks, he said, "I'll keep it with me and give it back to you when you come home. "

Unable to speak, trying not to break down and cry, I just smiled.

Jackie then watched as I was placed in the police car, and with our eyes glued to one another, I was driven away.

The police took me to a sanitarium in downtown Sacramento. It was a horrible experience. They took my clothes, gave me medication every two hours, and watched each move I made. They analyzed my artwork and made me explain them to a psychiatrist. I don't think he liked me very much, though, because I told him that my prayers were my confession. The only thing I had to talk to him about was getting out of that hospital and back to my son. Each day I looked forward to only two things: a visit from Jackie and the day I would get to go home.

On Sunday, December 12th, I received a visit from Jack and our son. Unfortunately, it wasn't full of the pleasure I had expected. As Jackie sat on my lap and talked about his daily activities, he asked, "Mommy, is my other Mommy better now?"

I thought it was rather strange that he would bring up the Avedikians out of nowhere, but I responded, "Yes, Jackie. Mary is much better."

He turned towards me, ran his fingers through my hair, and lowering his voice he said, "Then why can't I go home, Mommy?"

My heart dropped to my knees at hearing this. Was my absence making my son want to return to the Avedikian home? Guilt overwhelmed me, but before I could say a word Jackie whispered in my ear, "I don't want to move again Mommy."

I looked at Jack curiously, and he said, "Vickie, Jackie and I are moving to Los Angeles."

"You're what?"

"I have a better job waiting for me there."

"You can't!" I said loudly.

"I'll be driving cab still..." he whispered while looking around to see if attention was being drawn to us, "...but it's a full time job, and it pays better."

"I don't care what you have." I said as I clenched my teeth.

I held my son close and started to cry. Jackie knew that I was upset, and at first he sat very still and quiet. Then he tried to comfort me. He said, "Don't worry, Mom, when you're all better you can come and join us." He held up an item hanging from the chain around his neck, moved my hair out of eyes, looked and me and smiled, and said, "Until then, I have the ring, remember?"

I wiped my tears and nodded my head in agreement.

Jackie wrapped his arms around my neck and whispered, "I love you, Mom, and don't worry, it won't be long before I'll be giving you your ring back."

I held on tight to my son and sobbed.

When Jack and Jackie left that day, I fell into despair. I refused to get out of bed for a week and talked only to God. I thought a lot

158

about Jackie asking to return to the Avedikians, and I realized that my decision to have him near me by living with his father and giving him his family was actually making both of us terribly miserable. It was then that I decided I would go ahead and divorce Lloyd, even if it meant boarding Jackie again and returning to a life like we had before.

First, I had to find a way to get out of the hospital. I pulled myself together, called my parents, told them everything that had happened, and insisted they come and get me. Two weeks later, in January of 1950, I was back in Fresno again and living in my parents' home. At first everything was going well. I felt rejuvenated. I was actually excited about the decision I was making and anxious for my son and me to start over. I became diligent in my job seeking while also taking care of legal matters. I began the tedious paperwork necessary in filing for divorce from my husband and custody of my son.

I located Jack by calling all of the cab companies in Los Angeles. He told me that he was living with a woman, and that he had placed Jackie with welfare services.

Jack said, "I'm not going to tell you where he's at, but he's well taken care of."

I said, "Jack, you know I'm never going to harm my son."

"No, I don't know that," he said.

I begged him, "Please, at least meet with me?"

Jack was hesitant at first, but then agreed. I had little money so I took the inexpensive route and hitchhiked to Los Angeles. I waited all day at the place we agreed to meet, but Jack never showed. I tried to contact him by phone again, but they said he had gone home for the day. I returned home to Fresno that night without my son.

After two more months of attempting to locate Jackie and trying to find a job, I became desperate. I tried to pass the time by

Only Time

hanging out at my sisters' homes, but that was tough too because each of them had children, and I no longer had my son. Out of shame, I didn't contact any of my friends.

My family was as supportive as could be expected. My mother tried to assist by calling our Armenian relatives to see if they could help find me a job, but times were still tough for Armenians in Fresno, and they had nothing to offer. None of my siblings had anything to offer, with one asking, "What about your Armenian friends, can't they help you?"

My father had nothing but critical things to say. In fact, a young man named Tony came to Father for marital counseling, something I found in itself rather strange, and I overheard him say, "I have a daughter with the same problems, always worried about her family. I'll tell you the same thing I've always told her; if you're not happy, then leave."

It was a tough situation, living at home, not working, and not having any contact with my son. In early March, I decided to go back to Los Angeles again. This time I went directly to the cab-company where Jack worked, but I found that he was no longer employed there. I called everywhere and found nothing. I contacted the Welfare Department, but, due to safety concerns reported by his father, they refused to tell me the whereabouts of my son. I began to panic.

I returned to Fresno again, this time more distraught than I had ever been in my entire life. The peace, the truth, and the only love in my life were gone, and I couldn't find him.

On Wednesday, March 8th, I was in deep despair. I called my sister Angelique, and crying I asked her, "What will I do?"

She finally said, "Go to Los Angeles, get the boy, and I'll help you pay to board him out."

Blue Moon ...

By this point, I was a nervous wreck. Still unsure of what I might encounter going back to Los Angeles, my anxiety continued to build. By night I was overwhelmed and distressed. I had difficulty sleeping so Mother called the doctor who came to the house and gave me a shot to calm my nerves. I slept okay for the night, but my eyes popped open with the sun. I was still in a state of depression, feeling as though there was no hope for finding my son. Even if Angelique would help me pay to board Jackie out, I had no way of finding him, and no funds to continue seeking. Then, after tossing and turning for a couple of hours, I remembered that I had given my father money to hold for me.

I hopped out of bed and went into my father's office. I said, "I need the money I gave to you last year."

He asked, surprisingly, "What money?"

I was thrown back for a moment thinking that maybe I hadn't given it to him, or maybe he had already given it back to me. While my mind was racing through the past for a recollection of having already received the money, my father said, "That money you gave me you owed me!"

"Owed you? For what? Father, I need that money so I can get my son!" I said desperately.

"Even if you get him, you don't have a job to pay to have him boarded out, and he can't stay here. I told you before I'm not raising that man's son."

I was speechless. And that was it. I had had enough of my family's cruelty. I had to get out of there. And as I turned away I said, "I guess I better go somewhere and pray then."

He said, "Yes, you should."

Then I said, "Maybe you should join me..." as I continued to walk away. "I'll ask for help. You can repent."

I'd never spoken to my father in such a way, and I expected him to follow me with some form of punishment. But at this point I didn't even care. I walked into the bedroom and closed the door. I called Angelique, told her that I was hitchhiking to Los Angeles to find Jackie and hung up the phone before she could respond. I put on my coat, climbed out of the bedroom window, and began to walk. I turned off of our tiny street and down a main strip that led to the city and the highway that lead to my son.

All By Myself ...

10

SO, THAT'S THE TRUTH AS I KNOW IT, AND NOW I'M WALK-
ing down this road. I've passed the dirt, and the gravel, and now
I'm on the pavement. I can see and hear the sounds of cars zipping
by on the highway now. The noises have slowly gotten louder and
the buildings gradually bigger. And no one has bothered me. Maybe
it was the casual stroll I kept or my mind's obvious preoccupation.

This entire scene spurs a flood of memories. My sisters' and I
loved to hang out around here as children, and I had walks and
talks with Jack here when we were dating. The ballroom dance club
I frequented during my separation from Jack is here. The jobs I held
during my time as a single parent were here, and the transit system
that delivered me to my son each weekend used to pick me up here.
There were the walks with Little Jackie through the Courthouse Park,
picnics, swimming, roller-skating, pictures, movies, and the afternoon ice cream. I'm amazed at the size of this city now, how mas-

sive the structures have grown through the years. And that one, the Security Bank Building, with the lights and the cross. Oh, how I adored it so often in my late-night childhood prayers!

Where is my son? I just want to bring him home.

My heart is starting to race. I can't catch my breath. It's so dark. My eyes are closed so tightly I can't open them. I feel like my body is paralyzed. What's happening? Where am I? I don't feel like I'm even walking on a street. I feel like I'm sitting on something. My feet are dangling and my hands are locked, as if in prayer.

'Vickie, take the boy to the Avedikian home. It is best for now.'

'Vickie, Jackie and I are moving to Los Angeles.'

'Are you and Jack going to take him from us?'

"Miss, Miss, I'm in the window beneath you. I'm a police officer. Please come off the ledge and back inside the building?"

'If you're not going to speak English then don't speak at all.'

'You've been gambling, haven't you?'

'I have two dads and two moms.'

'You know we love this boy.'

'What money? That money you gave me you owed me.'

Oh my goodness...I'm falling. What's happening?

There, that's better. I can feel my legs now. I can breathe. I can open my eyes.

Oh, dear God, it's beautiful. It's just like I've always imagined, the mountains, the river, the valley, the scent of pine, and the breeze. Oh no, it's fading away. No, don't disappear.

'Until then, I have the ring, remember?'

Jackie?

'I love you, Mom, and don't worry, it won't be long before I'll be giving you your ring back.'

Jackie, hurry up, look at it before it's gone. Do you see it? It's Armenia.

Only Time

Part Three

Immortality

Fly ...

11

YES, GRANDMOTHER VICTORIA, HE SEES IT. THROUGH THIS story, we all see it. I'm sorry it took so long for me to hear your message and then find a way to respond, but quite often we listen only to the spoken words and not to what's being said silently. I know it's strange for me to stand here and talk to your headstone as though you can hear me, but your story has impacted and changed so many lives, it's the only place I could think of to come and tell you all that has happened.

GRANDMOTHER VICTORIA, NOT much changed after your death. Your family kept your funeral private and told the media only as much as they had to. They never told your mother how you died, and when your father's conscience got to him he tried to offer your husband money to leave Little Jackie with him and then for your husband to disappear. When your husband refused the offer and left Fresno with Little Jackie, your family was certain their secrets were safe. Or so they thought. I don't know if they ever realized there was still another branch of the family that was fully aware of, and sympathetic to, everything that happened during your life, and, of course, your death. These family members that your siblings had avoided throughout their lives, and others who knew you or witnessed your death, were more than willing to share your story with anyone curious enough to seek it.

After the newspaper article reported my search for answers into your suicide, your cousin Hagop contacted me. We talked on the phone, and he told me that you were the nicest of the Levon children, but because of the others' secrets and lies, you had it bad. He thought it was great that I was asking questions, but was quick to warn me that I wouldn't find any answers by asking your sisters. He said, "You're not going to get anything out of those girls. They've been lying their entire lives. They're not even French and Italian. They're Armenian."

It took a moment for my brain to actually hear and process the words that Hagop had just spoken. The concept of such a thing caught me completely off guard. Dad and I had never, ever, questioned our ethnic background, so I think I was in a state of shock to hear that. After a lifetime of responding to the 'Ethnicity Comments' and the 'Southern European' features, I was actually being told that I wasn't even French and Italian. Immediately I used this for a quick justification of one of my life's failures; I thought, 'Well, that explains the French classes in high school.'

And my response to him was one of obvious astonishment. When my mind finished registering exactly what had been said, and I pulled my chin off the floor, I asked him, at the truest level of ignorance, "What's Armenian?"

Up to this point, I had actually prided myself on being multi-culturally experienced and knowledgeable. Quite often in my life I was the ethnic minority in a variety of situations, but I could not relate to this one. I knew nothing about Armenia, its people, or its history and culture – or so I thought. When Hagop began to enlighten me on the history of Armenia, I started having flashbacks about a certain student from the speech class that initiated my family history research nearly a year and a half before. She talked about the genocide during WWI that I was surprised to have never learned about, and her grandparents' flight to the United States from the Turkish Government's attempted slaughter of their entire race of people. This student was Armenian. I was Armenian.

In discovering my own lack of knowledge about my family's true lineage, I decided to research Armenian history and current events. In effect, it gave me an awareness and pride in my heritage, as you had when you were alive. And, since I inherited the physical characteristics of your mouth, I decided to speak with it as you wished you could have, so I integrated it into my graduate studies.

I could have written a thesis comparing your story and Durkheim's theory on suicide, considering it actually did, contrary to what I initially thought, apply to you. But, I decided to look beyond the ties you did or did not have to a core value system or group, to the actual cause of your family's desire to abandon certain groups in favor of others. I studied race and ethnocentrism, immigration and adaptation, social class and structure. I examined nationalism: the devotion to a historically developed society that shares a common territory, lineage, language, economic life, and distinctive culture. With this, I used the Armenian paradigm and found that what your family, or what our family, did was not too unusual. Many Armenian immigrants had chosen to assimilate and acculturate into their adopted culture as much as possible by changing their names and their identities. Others had gone to the other extreme, completely rejecting the host country and refusing to sacrifice their traditions. Most, however, had fallen into the same category as you, somewhere in between, but I assume that most of these people also had someone to support them in the choice that they made.

While working on this thesis, I was also able to meet and interview numerous Armenian-American religious leaders, politicians, educators, and revolutionaries. One of those politicians, an Assemblyman, who had been touched by your story and impressed by the research I had completed, later presented me with a California Legislative Resolution. It stated that my hard work, "...epitomizes the accomplishments that Armenian Americans have made to California throughout its history by attending colleges and universities and becoming successful in a variety of professional endeavors and through community service." The Assemblyman then congratulated me on completing my Master's Degree.

I was thirty-one years old, and it was kind of strange to be suddenly recognized as an Armenian American, by an Armenian American. But it was a wonderful feeling to know that I belonged to such a proud and resilient group, and confirmation of the statement, 'Armenians know too well that nothing good or bad lasts forever, except for the being Armenian part, and that's good.'

I ALSO USED 'our' mouth to tell others in the family about our Armenian background. After talking to Hagop, I immediately contacted Dad. He and I just laughed. It was funny because we had long suspected that money was the issue that caused your sisters' fear of us, and to find that it was ethnicity was absolutely hilarious. Thinking about how long they were successful in hiding it, I can't imagine what type of laxative effect my curious nature must have

Immortality

created within them. The following day my Dad proudly told a friend, "I'm fifty-seven years old. Yesterday morning I woke up French and Italian, and at night I went to sleep Armenian."

When I called to share the news with Linda, she wasn't home, but her husband Steve answered the phone. I was disappointed that I couldn't tell her the news right at that moment, and I was too excited not to share the information with Steve. Later, when Linda walked into the house, Steve hugged and kissed her and said, "I've never kissed an Armenian before."

Linda later told me that she felt guilty because while growing up in Fresno people used to ask her if she was Armenian. Not knowing any better, she denied it. She also said that she used to wonder how her Grandma Anna knew how to make stuffed grape leaves. She said, "My mom always told me it was an Italian dish."

Linda has since had the honor of sharing the news with everyone else in the family. I wish I could have been a fly on the wall when she confronted your sisters. Of course they all denied knowing, even to the point of questioning the accuracy of our research. The younger generations are excited about it, though, yet at the same time they're upset at having been deceived by their parents. Everyone is busy, of course, developing his or her own theories behind the lies.

Overall, I imagine you would be happy to know that it's been a very welcome change within the family, and I've been able to establish wonderful relationships. Linda and I are close cousins now, and I recently vacationed in Greece with another cousin, your Uncle Krikor's granddaughter, Susie. Thank goodness she and her sister, Annette, don't have any hard feelings about what my great-grandfather did to their grandfather's blacksmith shop. And they still have the beaded picture of 'Mother Armenia' that your Mom and your aunts made in 1925 and then gave to your grandmother, Vartanoosh. It's hanging in their living room.

THERE IS ONE more event that took place that I must tell you about. I know the love that you had for your son and the concern you had for your family's lack of compassion towards him. But if there is a way, please be comforted in your death knowing that others have loved him in their place. First, there's my brother and I, and other family and friends. Then, there were others that we didn't know about, until now.

The day of the release of the newspaper article, two ladies contacted me. Over the phone they cried; they thanked me for a wonderful story, and they professed their forty-seven years of longing to know whatever happened to Little Jackie. As they described how they used to sit on their porch with your son, waiting for you to walk up the street to pick him up, one said, "Our names are Lena and Lydia. Our family's last name is Avedikian. Your father was our foster brother when he was a little boy."

Lena, said, "When I saw that picture of your grandmother in today's paper, and then I looked down at the picture at the bottom with him sitting on his mom's lap, I knew that was Little Jackie. That picture was taken in my front yard. My dad took that picture. I called my sister Lydia, who lives two doors down from me, the same house where our parents used to live, and I told her, 'Get up, get your paper. Little Jackie Smith is on the front page of the Life section.'

Then Lydia said, "I wasn't even dressed yet. I struggled to get some clothes on, and I grabbed my paper. When I opened it up, I started to cry." She said, "I've been going through old pictures of Little Jackie and crying all day."

"She told me that Noah's Ark alighted on Mt. Ararat, and when his family descended from the mountain and scattered throughout the world, some remained at the base of the mountain ... has become what we know as the Armenian people."

"It's been unfair for us children because we missed out on knowing our cousins."

"In 1925, when I was ten-years-old, Mother and her sisters made a picture out of beads ... at the bottom it was written, 'always love your motherland'."

Fly ...

Lena told me that they had always wondered what happened to Little Jackie. "He was like a toy to us," she said. "We used to hug him all the time, and he got so much love at our house. Our dad was very close to him and wanted to adopt him, but his mother wouldn't allow it. When Jackie was taken from our home, our dad used to cry. He died a short time later.

"But Jackie also had a great mother. She used to come to visit him every weekend, and she always brought him something. She loved Little Jackie very much. I remember she always kept herself neat, and she always looked so nice." Lena paused for a moment, and said, "She seemed sad, though."

Then Lydia added, "Every weekend when we waited on the porch with him, without fail his mom would come walking down that street. Jackie would start jumping up and down and yelling, 'Here comes my bus mommy, here comes my bus mommy.'"

Lydia told me that she had been going to school in San Francisco at the time of your death, and when her mom wrote and told of your suicide, she searched for Little Jackie. Lydia said, "I went to Los Angeles, and I tried to find him, but I couldn't. Our mother died just a few years later never knowing what happened to him."

"But now we know..." Lena said. "And I'm so excited. I went out to lunch with my friend today, and I couldn't stop talking about it. Even my friend got teary-eyed. Then, as we were leaving, there was a lady sitting at a table reading the article. I pointed at the lady's newspaper and said, 'That little boy used to live in my home'."

Then Lydia said, "Please bring him back to see us. You can stay with us. I have room at my house, and so does Lena, even if we all have to sleep on the floor. As long as we're all together."

Grandmother Victoria, this was quite an emotional phone call. Your sisters, my own blood relatives, told me that they had enough family. I'm certain that's the way they made you feel as well. But

Fly ...

the foster family was welcoming Dad and I, the same way they had opened their arms for the two of you so many years before. I was overwhelmed with emotion, silently joining them in their tears.

It took a few months, but yesterday I brought Little Jackie home. After checking into our hotel, which, coincidentally, is located across the street from the Armenian Church that your parents were married in ninety-seven years ago, we met Linda and her husband Steve here at the cemetery. Linda's first response when she saw Dad was, "Wow, you look just like a Levon!" We placed flowers on your grave and those of your parents' just a few feet away.

We also did some sightseeing, and you should have seen Little Jackie reminiscing. It was as though he was a little boy again. We drove past Angelique's old house, and he said, "I remember the train used to run behind the house. It was loud and the whole house would shake and wake me up out of my sleep. And I used to ride bikes with my cousins back in that alley."

We drove past your parents' old house, but the home we had seen in the pictures was gone and a newer one built in its place. From there we retraced your last steps into downtown Fresno. It was such an eerie sight to see that the city looked exactly the same as it had in the pictures that I'd seen from the time of your death. And as I stood at the base of the building from which you jumped, looking up at the same ledge, from the same angle as many of the witnesses had forty-seven years before, my body was in chills.

As we got back in our car and drove around downtown, Dad began to recall more of his childhood memories. He said, "That's where I learned to roller-skate. I wanted Mom to buy me some skates, but she wouldn't because I didn't know how to use them. I kept asking and she finally bought them." Laughing, he continued, "She brought me here and watched me fall until I learned to skate."

Then, as we drove by the courthouse he said, "Mom had an apartment right back here. Her drawings were all over the walls. The jailhouse was located over there on the side of the courthouse. Mom and I would always walk in between the two buildings. The prisoners would start hooting and howling, and Mom would try to act like she didn't hear them." Smiling, he paused and said, "I think she walked through there on purpose."

I didn't say a word. I just let him talk. These were memories he might not have recalled had we not come here, and I wanted him to enjoy it all.

We even drove past Elizabeth's old house, we saw the log cabin across the street that Grandpa Smitty, Uncle George, and Aunt Grace and Aunt Betty lived in when you met. Dad and I were surprised it was such a nice cabin, considering Grandpa Smitty's inability to keep job. Dad said, laughingly, "I would have expected it to be just a step up from a cardboard box."

Then we headed out to visit Lena and Lydia's. We turned down the same street you used to walk down from the bus stop. As we were looking at the homes for the correct address, we noticed an elderly lady standing in the front yard. It was Lydia anxiously awaiting our arrival. When we pulled up to the curb we waved and smiled, but before I could get myself out of the car and my get my video camera rolling, my dad was out of the car and once again in the arms of his foster sister, Lydia.

She pointed down the street to her house, the one dad lived in as a child, and then led us into Lena's house where the others were waiting. Lena was preparing dinner, and waiting to greet us was her other sister, Lucy, their brother Kerry and his wife Almeda, Lena's husband Bob, also Armenian, their daughter Renee, Renee's husband Scott, their daughter Natalie, Lydia's husband Karl, and their daughter, Kathy. It was amazing that so many people were there to see us. Also invited was Armine Lazarian, the other Armenian girl from the softball team who used to help baby-sit dad while you worked. She nearly made me cry when she walked up to Dad, and in a very soft voice said, "You look just like your father."

Then she walked straight over and hugged me. She drew back, and with tears in her eyes, looked at my face and right in my eyes as though I was you, and she hugged me again. It was an emotional moment, and I closed my eyes so that no one would see that I was beginning to cry.

They were all anxious to walk my dad through his childhood home in order to see what he could remember. Of course when we got there, we took a picture of him standing on the porch, as he did when he was a child awaiting your arrival. He remembered a lot about the home, and of course, having been a young boy when he lived there, most fondly remembered the back yard.

Back at Lena's house, we ate delicious Armenian food, and we talked with some of us fighting back tears. But the stories were worth telling: remembrances of a woman and her husband and softball. There were remembrances of a mother, a child, a desperate situation, and a loving family. There were moments of joy and times of tears.

After dinner we all talked some more and shared pictures. Lydia had saved some of my dad from when he was a child. My dad was shocked and asked me, "Are these pictures she saved or did you send them to her?"

I said, smiling, "No, Dad, she saved these."

There was a lot of discussion about our family, and as Linda was running off various names, some were familiar to Lena and Lydia's family. In fact, we found out that Lena's husband, Bob, knows your brother's son, Albert.

"I would always see him peering down the street in my direction … I couldn't understand exactly what was being said but I did hear the word 'mommy,' the only word that truly mattered."

"Our dad used to cry when he was taken from our home."

"Elisabeth's youngest daughter, Linda, was one of his favorites … she looked a lot like his Grandma Anna."

Fly …

Bob asked Linda, "Albert Levon is your cousin? We used to go to a Baptist church with a man named Albert Levon. His wife's name is Marie?"

She said, "Yes, that's him."

Then I spoke up and said, "He is one of the first people I contacted from the phone book when my research began. He was also one of those that was angry about my newspaper article."

Bob started laughing, and said, "Albert Levon, huh? He always passed himself off as being Portuguese."

Linda said, "Well, his mother, Elena, is Portuguese. But his father, my mother's brother, Peter, was Armenian."

Bob, with a sinister smile, said, "Next time I see Albert I'm going to ask him how the family is doing."

While the kids played for hours, the rest of us sat around talking, and a few of us ended up getting comfortable on the floor. As time passed, though, night was approaching, and we were all exhausted. We said our farewells, with promises of future contact, and returned to our hotel for a good night sleep. This morning when we awoke I decided I wanted to stop here again before we left town. I had Dad drop me off, and I sent he and the girls over to the florist to get you some more flowers, so that I would have time to talk to you. I see they're coming back now so I have to wrap it up.

Grandmother Victoria, now that I know you, I certainly could never forget you. I wear the ring to keep both you and your son close to my heart. And I will always pray for your soul, in hopes that on the day Little Jackie has to leave this life, God might allow you to be waiting for him at the gates of heaven. Go ahead now, take your love and fly, find a place to rest.

Fly ...

"Recently I told my mom that I wished I could remember my Aunt Vickie and my grandparents better... still the memories are good ones."

"I also thought a lot about my grandmother having lived as an actual being."

"...when we were sitting in the driveway he told me that Mom was dead. I was ten-years-old ... we didn't get to stay for mom's funeral."

Fly ...

We Belong Together ...

12

IF I COULD TURN BACK THE HANDS OF TIME, I WOULD. MY dad would have the irreplaceable experience of a lifetime with a mother to nurture him, and I would have the joy of a grandmother to spoil me, disregard all of my parents' rules, and allow me to do things my dad wasn't permitted to do as a child. Unfortunately, I can't touch time. All I can do is take advantage of the future and attempt to correct the misdeeds of the past.

This experience has left me thinking of many things: family, ethnic identity, faith, and the value we place on each. If Emile Durkheim's theory is correct and we do need to be members of some type of group that will bind us to our value system, then I believe that these would definitely be the most important ones. Whether blood relative or not, we need family to forgive, understand, and unconditionally love and support us. Ethnic or cultural identity is

186

important, because the bonds within a society that are created, transformed, and strengthened through time give people a system of traditions to bind together in groups of custom and familiarity. Especially important is faith, because believers in Christianity can call on Jesus for strength and mercy in this life, as well as salvation of their eternal souls.

Personally, I think my grandmother understood the importance of these groups as well, as she tried so desperately to hold on to even the smallest piece of each. Unfortunately, she was also alone in this attempt, powerless in her connections. She was abandoned by her family, severed from traditional religious guidance, and forbidden from strengthening ties with her heritage. Then, when she lost the only one to whom she had an intense bond, Little Jackie, her spirit was ultimately killed. The only thing left of Victoria was the hollow shell of a woman, whose last act was to raise a red flag.

TODAY, MY LIFE is as it has always been, busy. I'm finished with school, for now, and I work and take care of my children. My grandmother's sisters still have no desire to be in contact with me, but the other relatives do. Lena and Lydia, and their families, are still wonderful friends – teaching me Armenian culture and how to cook Armenian food – which I then pass on to my children. Lena's husband, Bob, and I discuss Armenian history and political issues. I also immerse myself in Armenian related issues whenever possible.

I have been welcomed into, and enjoy the local Sacramento Armenian community, and my brother and I recently created a Sacramento Armenians Web Site. Also, I began a research, community outreach, and education association, in honor of my grandmother, in which I am currently extracting the demographics of Armenians from Census Records, in hopes of creating a database for genealogi-

Immortality

cal research assistance. My grandmother felt it was something worth dying for; I consider it something worth living for. I work for the memory of my grandmother and the future of Armenians.

I DON'T REMEMBER being told about my grandmother's suicide; it's just one of those things it seems I've always known. I do, however, remember the first image I created of her. I pictured a lady standing near the edge of a building top, late at night in a small desert town. No one else was around, just me standing on the sidewalk below. I watched for a few moments from the base of the building, then decided to get a closer look. I floated off the ground to a height just above where she stood and began to circle around. I noticed that the dress she was wearing, and her black, shoulder-length hair was flowing back from a slight breeze. Occasionally I would zoom in closer, hoping to see some type of emotional expression, but finding none, I drew back to a more comfortable distance. All the while there was complete silence—only the sound of my thoughts.

Becoming more curious about this lady and her intentions, I stopped circling above and stood by her side. First, I looked directly at her face, hoping she would turn and acknowledge my presence. But she never looked my way, continuing instead to stare straight ahead into the distance.

Wondering what it was that captivated her so, I looked out the same direction and saw the outskirts of this town. To my surprise, though, the darkness had turned to light, and instead of seeing a dry and empty desert, I was standing next to my grandmother overlooking the most beautiful, colorful valley I'd ever seen. Rays of the sun shimmered across the surface of a rolling river that flowed from the range of snow-capped mountains lining this vast plain of lush green grass and array of colorful wild flowers. It was a beautiful valley, a sight of magnificent splendor. In the midst of the fear and

We Belong Together...

concern that I felt while watching my grandmother, it was a vision that somehow comforted me and resonated a delicate peace and serenity.

As my grandmother and I watched the earth adorning herself, I began to feel a strange sensation beneath my feet. I glanced down to find myself standing alone, without any shoes, in a mass of rich soil and what I believed was the soul of grass and flowers. I looked up to find that I had joined this landscape. The eternal sky soared above me and the silence of my image was pleasantly interrupted by the angelic notes of birds in flight showering a rain of melody. I could smell the fragrance of the land that surrounded me, each of the flowers in bloom and the scent of pine from the trees. A soothing breeze whispered in my ear as it exhaled over the meadow.

It was a splendid vision that gave me an immense sense of euphoria, and after basking for a moment, I leaned down to pluck a flower from its stem. I had hoped to turn back and offer it to my grandmother so that she might also inhale its breath and revel in the same sweetness of nature as I. Forty-seven years later, I did.

The memories of this entire experience are sweet ones, and there will now forever be new significance to my name, more relevance to my physical features, and more irony in my initial reaction to my dad's resemblance to his mother, "You have her nose. Look, Dad, that's your nose."

"I could use the speech as an excuse to finally ask the questions I'd wanted to ask virtually my entire life."

EPILOGUE

SO MUCH CHANGE HAS TAKEN PLACE SINCE THAT FATAL day in Fresno. The population has more than doubled, and though the downtown area has retained much of the skyline that would be familiar to Victoria, she would never recognize the sprawling suburbia that has surrounded and engulfed much of the former rich farmland. Shopping malls and restaurants are just as much a part of the scenery as the vineyards. Prominently standing across from the Holy Trinity Armenian Church Victoria's parents attended, now is a proud landmark for all Armenians—the William Saroyan Theater, next to the Fresno Convention Center. And in recent years, Fresno has witnessed the influx of many Armenian immigrants from the former Soviet Union, all in search of the American dream, just as those immigrants of Victoria's day.

In Armenia, the pitiful population went through the prolonged national nightmare of the Stalin era and the added horrors of the Second World War. After years of misery, starting in the 1960's the Armenians in Soviet Armenia slowly started to advance in life in the sense of having more than just the necessities of life. The following decade saw improvements in the quality of life of the average Armenian, with much development of cities and the industrial sections of the country. The 1980's brought the most prosperous times for Soviet Armenia. Every family had a 'chicken in the pot' so-to-speak, and many enjoyed the luxury of an automobile. Though suppressed by American standards, there was enough prosperity to go around for every family. As in the case of all other Soviet Satellite countries, Armenia learned the ins and outs of existence under Communism—people knew how to get what they wanted one way or another. Poor and modest by Western European and American standards, they all had enough to eat and enjoyed unprecedented prosperity in Soviet history—especially compared to other Communist countries such as Red China, and even other Soviet satellite countries.

This state of euphoria came to an alarmingly abrupt halt in ways no one dreamed of. Along with April 24, 1915 (the commemorative date of the Armenian Genocide), December 7, 1988 is one of the most tragic and dreaded dates for all Armenians. On that day an intensely devastating earthquake took more than 100,000 lives in Armenia. To this day, many parts of devastated Armenia still have not been rebuilt, and some bodies have as their tombstones, the rubble of wrecked buildings. Soon after that natural disaster, the Soviet Union dismantled, leaving the satellite countries in uncertainty. There was the tantalizing prospect of American style democracy and prosperity as fantasized by many who desired to emigrate to America, but Armenia, along with the other nations, was totally unprepared to make the transition. The hapless Armenians of their newly independent and free country, also had to contend with the costly conflict with neighboring Azerbaijan. It was and continues to be costly in terms of lives lost and meager funds spent on munitions. Armenian Democracy was economically prosperous for too few, and for the majority of people, the future is economically and politically bleak with ominous dark clouds on the horizon. As a result, more than one million Armenian nationals have departed the country to America, Europe and throughout the former Soviet Union in search of economic stability and survival.

Armenia entered the threshold of the third millennium with much uncertainty. But then, uncertainty is the ever-present reality in the world of Armenia. As in the past, we depend on God, waiting to see the hope we have placed on Him, shine brilliantly through the dark and ominous clouds once more, and to preserve the ancient land of Noah, the cradle of civilization and its people.

Presently, worldwide celebrations are underway to mark the 1700th anniversary of the declaration of Armenia as the first Christian nation in world history. May God Almighty honor the faith of Armenians, and preserve our nation and people as long as there is life on this planet.

Father Yeghia Hairabedian

ACKNOWLEDGEMENTS

Support through a project such as this comes in many forms. To my dad, thank you for your wisdom. To my mom, thank you for your unconditional love. My children, Courtney, Moriah, and Jordan, thank you for your understanding. To my brother, Alan, thank you for all the time you invested. Aunty Carolyn, you are an inspiration of strength, Honey. Thank you to my cousins, Steve and Linda, for your love and acceptance, and Annette and Susie, thank you for being so much fun. Thank you to the Avedikian children, our foster family, and their families, for extending love and kindness to our family. To my friends, Kim Andersen, Veronica Hackett-Cole, Veronica Freeman, Angelique Jean, and Ellen Brown, thank you for years of daily encouragement. To Chris Zachariou, thank you for loaning me your intellect, and thank you for active involvement each step of the way. Jonathan and Jennifer Zachariou, thank you for your spiritual guidance. To Dean Foston, thank you for the provisions in the early stages of my research. Thank you to my graduate professor's, Robert Kloss and Andre Rendon, for overseeing my thesis while understanding my unique circumstance. Ara Movsessian and Arra Avakian, thank you for your advice. To Jane Beal (my 'comma mamma'), thank you for your editing skills. A special thanks to Father Yeghia Hairabedian for your confidence in my abilities, your enthusiasm, and for all of your assistance (as I'm your favorite blonde, you're my favorite priest). Special thanks extends to Father Hairabedian's congregation at the Sacramento St. James Armenian Church, and the rest of the Sacramento Armenian Community as well. Thanks to anyone else whose life has crossed with mine in the past four years and who stopped to offer their time and assistance with this project. Most importantly, thank you God for providing me, first, with this path, and then the feet to walk it.

197

SOURCES AND SELECTED BIBLIOGRAPHY

Adalian, Rouben Paul. (1995). Remembering and Understanding the Genocide. Yerevan, Armenia: National Commission of the Republic of Armenia on the 80th Commemoration of the Armenian Genocide.

Avakian, Arra S. (1998-2000). Armenia: A Journey Through History. Fresno, California: The Electric Press.

Crittenden, Jules. (December 2000). "Origins of Things Armenian." Armenian International Magazine.

Kulhanjian, Gary A. (1975). An Abstract of the Historical and Sociological Aspects of Armenian Immigration to the United States, 1890-1930. Cambridge, Massachusetts: Harvard University Press.

Lang, David Marshall. (1981). The Armenians: A People in Exile. London: George Allen & Unwin.

Mirak, Robert. (1993). Torn Between Two Lands: Armenians in America, 1890-WWI. Cambridge, Massachusetts: Harvard University Press.

Paskerian, Charles R. (September 5, 1992). "The Armenians: A Brief History." The Orange County Chapter, Triple X Fraternity.

Salt, Jeremy. (July 1990). "Britain, The Armenian Question, and The Cause of the Ottoman Reform." Middle Eastern Studies. Vol. 26; No. 3.

Suny, Ronald Grigor. (1993). Looking Toward Ararat: Armenia in Modern History. Cambridge, Massachusetts: Harvard University Press.

Tootikian, Vahan H. (1998). Pastoral Meditations. Southfield, Michigan: Armenian Heritage Committee.

Zachariou, Philemon. (1999) The Proselytizer. ACW Press: Phoenix, Arizona.

http://www.thehistorynet.com/militaryhistory/articles/12963. The History Net. "Armenian Christians." November 8, 1998.